Talking About
Isa

Sharing Jesus with Your Muslim Friend

Talking About Isa
Sharing Jesus with Your Muslim Friend
by James Bryanson

Copyright © 2016 by James Bryanson
All Rights Reserved
1st Edition

Edited by Kelli Sallman

Perfect Bound Edition
ISBN-13: 978-0-9988494-0-9

Electronic Edition
ISBN-13: 978-0-9988494-1-6

Scripture quotations taken
from the New American Standard Bible® (NASB),
Copyright © 1960, 1962, 1963, 1968, 1971, 1972, 1973,
1975, 1977, 1995 by The Lockman Foundation
Used by permission. www.Lockman.org

info@hispubg.com

Contents

Preface	5
Introduction	9
1. Test the Waters	13
2. Everywhere You Look	23
3. Not So Easy Access	29
4. Find an Imam	37
5. Make a "Close" Friend	49
6. No Room at the End	65
7. Island Hopping	79
8. Refugee Camp Reprieve	87
9. Shop Owner Story Time	97
10. Imam's Unlikely Chant	107
11. Member of Parliament and the Trinity	113
12. Dinner with a Friend's Friend	117
13. The Whole Truth with No More Rebuttal	127
14. Eggs Lead to Eternal Life	137
Conclusion	145
Appendix A: Glossary of Terms	151
Appendix B: Acts 17	157

Appendix C: Call to Prayer   159

Appendix D: Surah 1, Holy Qur'an   161

Appendix E: Qurban Poster   163

Appendix F: Abraham's Story from Qur'an   165

Appreciation   167

Preface

I'm delighted that you are willing to read a book about Isa. I want to say at the onset, ***this book is not written for your Muslim friend.*** Rather, it is written for Followers of Jesus to understand Muslim culture and to adopt the vocabulary and skills necessary to have a conversation with them about Jesus.

Talking About Isa provides real world examples of the kind of conversations that begin to change the view of Jesus in a Muslim's eyes. These talks frequently do not complete the whole picture of salvation in one sitting. Muslims often are open to only one key piece of the puzzle being placed on the table at a time. Having an understanding that you cannot take your audience beyond where they are willing to go is paramount when working with those from an Islamic background.

Sometimes you find a person who gravitates to understanding, assembles the pieces very quickly, and comes to saving faith in Jesus. They become aware instantly that their works are incapable of overcoming their sins. As you might have guessed, these quick responders are, by far, the minority. In all cases, we should avoid making our focus the Muslim's response to salvation. If we have presented the truth as clearly and in accordance with their own world view as possible, then we have made ourselves available to wade into the water with them as deep as they are able to go.

Letting go of your own culture's vocabulary and vehicles for delivering truth can be a difficult task. Paul's monumental speech before the Athenians in Acts 17:22–31 is the quintessential example (see Appendix B). Paul would have known the Torah—the first five books of the Bible—by memory and had an in-depth understanding of the books of the prophets. It is important to note that he chose not to use his culture, vocabulary, or sources in this speech.

Instead of quoting from his holy books, explaining Jesus from a Jewish background and Jewish traditions, Paul chose to complement his audience's own understanding of God. As a bridge, he used the Athenian's altar to an unknown god and quoted from their pagan poets.

I could have included in this book a dozen stories of Muslims saying 'Yes' to Jesus. That would have been a very uplifting book. However, that would have left you with the wrong expectation as well as missed the opportunity to show you how to resist pushing on a door that isn't ready to open. **For those reasons and others, these stories are primarily about Muslims who not did come to faith (at least not that I'm aware).**

The following stories are meant to explain how to draw from as many bridges as possible within the Islamic world view. This is so you may know how to teach clearly that Jesus (*Isa al Masih*) is the only way to God (*Allah*).

Every clear gospel presentation has something about sin, something about the Savior, and something about faith/trust. As you read this book, I would invite you to keep a mental checklist of these three components and see how far each conversation goes.

A glossary, located in the back of the book, will add clarification to many Islamic terms. Most of their meanings will soon become evident from the content. "PBUH" means Peace Be Upon Him. Try to say the full words to yourself every time you see the acronym. It is the most respectful way to mention a prophet.

—James

Talking about ISA

Introduction

The art of contextualization has always been a heavily debated topic. The disagreement is largely because every culture thinks theirs is the only correct culture, especially those who have several generations of Christianity behind them. The practice of how we express our faith, and even how we present the gospel, can become codified to the point that we feel all other cultures must come to faith using the the same terminology and methods that we did.

Stripping away American culture from the gospel is not only effective, it's biblical. If American missions are making disciples internationally that look like us, talk like us, dress like us, and worship in our language, then we have failed. We have exported a lifestyle and a culture, not a Savior.

Of course, this struggle is not new. In Acts 15 at the Jerusalem Council, the early church had to wrestle with how far to bend for Gentile converts. The urge was to make them culturally like a Jew. Thankfully, the elders and the apostles realized that it was not a subculture that makes people true followers of Jesus, but rather the One in whom they trust to be their intermediator.

The point of this book is to wrap the gospel in terms that make sense and, as clearly as possible, present Jesus to Muslims in a way that they are able to receive Him. Not for them to receive a North American denomination. Not for them to receive another culture's view of the world. Not for them to receive a new religion. Rather, to see the person of Jesus and his finished work on their behalf.

The gospel, clearly and biblically defined according to 1 Corinthians 15:3–4, is that Christ died for our sins and on the third day rose from the dead. If you were raised in a Christian tradition, that statement makes perfect sense to you. That's because from a very young age, you were familiarized with the concept of substitutionary atonement.

However, if you were raised in an Islamic tradition, that statement would be the most absurd thing you have ever heard. First, what does someone else's death have to do with you? Second, why would God allow one of his prophets to be shamed that way? These ideas are foreign concepts that must be explained.

An even more difficult concept for them is putting Jesus in a category above prophethood. In order to have an atoning sacrifice, it is necessary that the sacrifice offered not be bound by the same problem as the one for whom it atones. For example, if you are a prisoner and need to post bond, your bondsman cannot be imprisoned as well. He must not be in the same predicament. In the same way, Christ would not have been able to take the place of sinners if he himself were a sinner. Muslims believe that only Allah is sinless. The Messiah would need to be spotless, clean, and holy like no other man who ever walked earth. Jesus is more than the prophet they have come to know him as.

So after establishing the nature of Christ, we must teach substitutionary atonement, the idea that someone can die in place of someone else. This must be done in a culturally relevant way—and through story if the people group are circular thinkers rather than linear.

Lastly, we must offer people the opportunity to receive this sacrifice on their behalf, letting go of the good works they were previously trusting in to make them clean.

Not an easy task. It is no wonder that there are still more than six thousand unreached people groups, almost half of which, according to the Joshua Project, are

Muslims. We have very few workers currently engaged in reaching them—about one full-time worker for every one million Muslims.

Traditional methods of sharing the gospel will not work. Not because they do not hold truth, but because they are delivering the truth in a way that cannot be understood. I do not offer this book as *the* answer but as *an* answer that is bearing fruit.

Chapter 1

Test the Waters

The first year I began practicing Muslim outreach, I vowed I would never stay in another Christian guesthouse while traveling internationally. That decision landed me at a Somali hotel just up the street from one of the largest mosques in the city. This small, three-story establishment, built with only a small, gated side-entrance, was laid out in a simple fashion with a very small reception area. The front desk shared its space with the foot of the stairs. As there was no elevator, I dragged my carry-on, laptop bag, and checked luggage up two narrow flights of stairs to the next floor.

    The first stay was a bit nerve racking. I guessed, by the occasional wide-eyed stares, that not many Anglo-Americans frequented the hotel. It only took a few visits, however, and I became known on a first name basis. I could even make my reservation by sending the manger a text the week before arriving.

It was on my first visit that I decided if I couldn't walk into a mosque and present the gospel, there was no reason to be in my line of work. Nor could I train anyone else to do what I had not done myself. So off I went to the mosque late one afternoon.

I knew little about prayer postures, order of worship, or even which way to face. It must have seemed a bit odd to the local participants to see me walk in the gate that day, take off my shoes, and go inside to sit down in the mostly empty prayer hall. Evening prayers were still several hours away, and very few Muslims, if any, come to read the Qur'an or have extra prayers.

During my third visit to this mosque, after praying in a not-so-Islamic prayer posture, the imam took me aside and explained what I was doing wrong. Then, I went back outside and immediately found three Somalis in starched-white *thobes*, complete with checkered headdress, standing in a circle.

I boldly approached them and said, "I've just come from Dubai, and I'm hearing many stories from people returning from *hajj* that are having visions and dreams of a prophet. Have you ever had a dream or vision of a man clothed in white?"

After a brief conversation among themselves, one turned and said, "No, we haven't. But you need to speak to that man over there." Turning to look where they were pointing revealed an elderly Somali man with a long beard, who was sitting on the curb observing our conversation.

He watched my impersonal introduction from a distance and noticed my approach to a place next to him under the shade of a large tree in the late afternoon African sun. I raised my question to him about having a dream or vision of a man in bright white robe.

There was a slight pause, which caused me to wonder whether he understood what I was asking or if he even spoke English. Clarity on the matter came quickly as he broke the silence with a perfectly clear English accent, "No, I have not, but why do you ask?"

"Well, I think I know who he is. He is found in the third *surah* of the Qur'an." I kept on speaking, for fear of more questions. "It says beginning at *aya* 42 that Isa al Masih, peace be upon him (PBUH), was born of a virgin named Maryam. It continues to say that Masih Isa (PBUH), had the power to heal the blind man, the ability to raise the dead, and the ability to create life."

Proud of myself that I had gotten that much out in a mosque courtyard, I turned my gaze upward to see several tall men heading my direction. To my surprise, they weren't armed and neither were they upset. A crowd of eight had gathered in a semicircle to hear the stranger's story. The only problem now was that I wasn't prepared for a crowd, so I quickly forgot my place within my story. Drawing a blank, I looked back at my elderly counterpart on the sidewalk in hopes of drawing some inspiration.

Skipping the entire middle of the presentation, I picked up at the close: "There are three *qurban* that Allah has offered. The first was offered for Adam (PBUH) when Adam ate the forbidden fruit and was thrown out of paradise." Then I boldly added an interpretation: "For only one sin, the first prophet was not able to walk with Allah in paradise."

What happened next was as equally surprising as the crowd wanting to listen. To my left, a much shorter and darker-skinned man turned to his taller counterpart and said clearly in their local language, "What the white man is saying is that it only takes one sin to keep you out of paradise." I was awed at the insight he grasped so quickly. I did not expect such understanding in such a short amount of time, and to hear it verbalized for all in attendance was incredible.

Because I was doing my presentation in English, I continued on, pretending not to have understood his statement made in the local dialect. "The second qurban was given to Ibrahim (PBUH) after he passed the test of faith to sacrifice his son on a mountain. Of course we know he did not kill him. Instead, Allah provided a qurban in place of his son. Since there was a ram caught in the bushes, Allah said to Ibrahim that he should not kill his son, but offered the ram instead. That is because Allah can provide substitute qurban—something to die in place of someone else.

Once again, all words left me. It was as if all the floodgates of a dam closed without notice, and all thoughts instantly stopped flowing. I looked down at my watch and then at my small audience, and I mumbled something about getting back to my hotel for my next meeting.

As I stood to leave, I braced myself for rebuttal, critique, or correction. But it never came. I slowly made my way toward the gate as the group followed. They asked when I could come back to tell more stories. They also inquired where I was staying, which appropriately was a Muslim hotel. Then one of them asked to join me for breakfast the next day.

At first, these efforts to share the gospel seemed to me like a failed attempt. But over time, I began to see a picture about how to talk about Isa take shape.

Implications

To the Western reader, talking about a book called the Qur'an, speaking about animals being killed for qurban, and wishing peace on prophets sound very odd. For the evangelical, these words can feel even unbiblical. The idea of entering a mosque and participating in Muslim prayer time can be very unnerving.

A mosque is simply a place where people gather to offer pre-memorized prayers to the Creator (see Appendix D). The minaret that often adorns the top of a mosque may have been borrowed from Orthodox churches. There are no idols in a mosque or any carved images. All are forbidden since they distract from the worship of the one true God.

The prayer postures Muslims go through during their act of submission means they have come to

- hear from God;
- receive fullness;
- bow to his glory;
- ask for forgiveness;
- give God praise; and
- profess and affirm that God is the greatest.

When performing this ritual, it is not done before an altar, to a prophet, or to an image. It is done facing Mecca because that city is believed to be the holiest place on earth since the Prophet Muhammad was born there.

Most evangelicals don't get an uncomfortable feeling when they drive past a Jewish synagogue. They sense that what is going on inside is the root of their own faith, and it seems somehow benign. But if they were to go into the synagogue and begin asking question about *Yeshua Mashiach* (Messiah Jesus), they would quickly find that their line of questioning was considered blasphemy.

Yet the same conversation with anyone in a mosque brings a much different response. Isa al Masih (Jesus the

Messiah) is the second most revered prophet in the Qur'an. He is mentioned by name twenty-five times and referred to 104 times in total. Jesus is also called

- the Word of God;
- the One closest to God;
- the Truth; and
- the Spirit of God.

It may seem disturbing to say in a mosque that Jesus was born of a virgin and has power over sickness and death. But reciting these words from the Qur'an takes away any friction and opens an incredible dialogue.

At the same time, showing that Adam could not overcome even one sin and that God provides substitute sacrifices may sound to a Western ear as no big deal. Yet for the Muslim, they are essential notions to make clear. Both of those concepts, that you cannot overcome your sins through good works (prayers, hajj, giving, etc.) and that God provides a substitute sacrifice, are contrary to Islamic theology. Yet Muslims are very open to hearing about these concepts and stories that originated in the Bible when they are taught through the Qur'an.

Of course, even though these truths exist in their holy book, it doesn't make followers of Islam a part of the Messianic Kingdom. What it does make possible is the means to explain about following Isa (Jesus) within an Islamic environment.

Talking about ISA

Chapter 2

Everywhere You Look

Frequent trips in and out of the country put me often in major airports at the last port of call before leaving North America. Sitting at a gate once, I noticed a brown-skinned man, whom I presumed to be Ethiopian, approach a table for charging electronic devices and take a seat.

I proceeded to reposition myself and take a seat next to him. Always eager to use the only word I know in another language, I said, "*Ahmah-segah-nalu*," which in Ethiopian means "thank you."

He politely smiled back and said in well-learned English, "Thank you, but I'm not Ethiopian. I'm Somali."

"Somali," I exclaimed. "You are the first Somali I've ever met in this city. *Asalaam wa aleikum.*"

"*Aleikum salaam*," came his eager reply.

I asked how long he had been in the States, where he worked, and where he lived. He was actually at his job then, just on break. He stocked shelves at the newsstand located just opposite from where we were sitting. I also learned that I was the first follower of Jesus to speak with him since he had arrived five years before.

I reached into my carry-on bag and pulled out my English-Arabic Qur'an that an imam had given me in an Egyptian mosque. As I laid it on the table, I asked, "May I share with you my favorite passage from the Qur'an?"

"Of course," he said, his surprise reverberating back. Imagine his delight in finding a nonimmigrant American who not only smiled at him rather than glare with distrust, but also spoke to him and wanted to share with him from a book that he had been taught to respect from his childhood.

"It says in *Al-Imran*, right here," I said, pointing to the beginning of the passage, "that Masih Isa (PBUH) was very special since he was born of the virgin Maryam. This is important for several reasons but the most important has to do with the fact that there is only one other prophet that had no earthly father: Adam (PBUH). Adam walked with Allah in paradise until something went wrong. And when that event happened, the children of Adam began killing one another. The problem, which Adam started, passed on from generation to generation to all of the descendants of Adam up until now. Everyone in the line of Adam got Adam's problem. That is, all except one: Isa al Masih (PBUH).

"This one difference in Masih Isa (PBUH) is the key to his sinless and holy nature. He did not have an earthly father, so he did not have the same problem that every other person in the line of Adam (PBUH) had been given by his or her father.

"The reason he had to be sinless and holy is connected to the way Allah covers sin and shame, namely qurban, or sacrifice. You see, there must be a covering for sin and shame for us to be allowed into paradise. Adam (PBUH) was removed from being in Allah's paradise because of the sin and shame he had when he ate of the forbidden fruit.

"Surah 20:121 says, 'Then they both ate thereof, so that their nakedness became manifest to them, and they began to cover themselves with the leaves of the garden. And Adam observed not the commandment of his Lord, so his life became miserable.'

"Adam tried to cover his own problem. Notice Allah's response: 'But Allah said, O ye Children of Adam! We have bestowed raiment upon you to cover your shame, as well as to be an adornment to you. But the raiment of righteousness—that is the best. Such are among the Signs of Allah, that they may receive admonition!' (7:26).

"We can't fix our problem. Only Allah can. The greatest fix Allah provided was spoken of in the third chapter of the Qur'an. This is where the prophet Muhammad (PBUH) in Al-Imran, aya 55 explained, 'Lo!' God said, 'O Jesus! Verily, I shall cause thee to die, and shall exalt thee unto Me.' Allah offers Masih Isa (PBUH), the blameless Holy Lamb, as a qurban. He did this to remove our sin and our shame.

"After performing qurban, he raised Isa from the dead and had Isa travel the straight path to paradise. Allah did this so that anyone who wanted to receive the qurban that he provided, could have their sin and shame removed and be guaranteed a place in paradise. Would you like to receive the qurban of Isa so you can go to paradise?"

I held my breath and braced for the onslaught of verbal backlash I assumed I was sure to receive in return. After all, you don't just tell a Somali Muslim that his guaranteed way to heaven is through Jesus and not the five pillars, right?

He looked me square in the eyes and said, "Yes, I understand I must have the qurban of Isa in order to enter paradise. I want to receive him." I was once again dumbstruck. Then it dawned on me that he had just realized his sin couldn't be overcome by the pillars of Islam, and he was receiving the payment of Jesus. I had never seen this happen before, and I wanted to jump up in the room full of waiting passengers and explain that this Somalian just understood the gospel.

I exchanged phone numbers with him and watched as he returned to the newsstand where he stocked the shelves.

Implications

Paul was master of culture and communication. In addition, he had the equivalent of a PhD in the Old Testament. His command of the Torah as a Pharisee would have been second to none. His devotion to the text and the resulting rules were innate to his world view.

All of these points make his sermon on Mars Hill in Acts 17 (see Appendix B) all the more remarkable. We would expect Paul to "preach the Word" (2 Tim. 4.2). After all, it is scripture that changes people, right?

Well, yes and no. The Greek polytheistic society Paul was addressing had neither knowledge of his scriptures nor respect for them. Quoting or executing concepts that were foreign to the world view of his audience would have created further misunderstanding. He had no recourse but to use biblical truth—but only that which he could stitch together from within the Greek society where he found himself.

When Paul wrote that to the Jews he became as a Jew, and to those without the law he became like those without law so that he might win some (1 Cor. 9:20, 21), he was by no means falsely claiming to hold their beliefs. Nor did he fail to correct them where they were errant. With great skill he used what was available within the culture to teach biblical truth; this method was similar to Jesus's use of parables. To construct his message, he drew from that which was familiar to his audience.

Paul created a bridge to Jesus from a nearby altar to an unknown god, and he quoted from a pagan poet. He never even quoted from his own holy book. It is paramount to begin where your audience is within their own world view in order to move them to the new world view that God desires they adopt.

Chapter 3

Not So Easy Access

The '92 Prado being prepped for wrapping with a giant sticker required a washing from top to bottom, inside and out. A Prado is an African– and Middle-Eastern-marketed, box-shaped, Toyota 4X4. We needed a sales truck for our project to get low-emission cooking stoves into an unreached people group, and the manager's personal Prado would do nicely.

We took it to a local gas station that had a car wash bay. It wasn't far from the Somali hotel where we had spent the night, eaten a remarkable, perfectly spiced meal, and joked with many of the staff. A group of Anglo-Americans, we were certain to be conspicuous in the neighborhood. We were hidden in plain sight.

As we began the washing process by removing the near permanent red haze left by the iron-rich soil, we noticed that others in the garage took a great interest in our work. Modeling is always the best way to change behavior. I often say that people don't do what they hear others saying; they do what they see others doing.

After the initial full car wash, which would have looked like any other hand-wash job, we then set to detail the car. We had to remove the most infinitesimal specks of dirt in the tiniest cracks so that the large 3M vehicle sticker would adhere firmly to the body. So we set about eliminating the finely collected dust from every seam of the vehicle. We even used toothbrushes.

As we progressed to the door jams, the creases created by trim, and the welded joints, we noticed that our onlookers had grabbed the extra toothbrushes we had left around the perimeter. They took our cue and began washing their cars in a similar fashion. We all smiled widely at this unnecessary adherence to our methods for their ordinary car wash.

There was a lot of effort to detail and clean this old 4x4. It was a long process and drew a lot of attention on a busy Saturday morning at this particular gas station. It was a spectacle, for certain, to see Americans outside their homeland washing a vehicle with the microtenacity of a

Swiss watchmaker. None of this activity, however, led to us being able to announce ourselves as followers of Jesus. It was the inadvertent work of my older brother that pulled off this last feat.

It was his first trip outside the United States. He was doing stellar. Respectful, polite, and willing to try anything new—including three-day-old camel milk in a smoke-lined gourd—he always made sure to ask before doing anything that might have potentially unknown consequences. When he asked if he could take some photos around the venue, I had no hesitation answering. This particular country was well accustomed to tourists with cameras.

So as my older brother walked out of the car wash area into the bustle of humanity refueling, he entered into chaos: cars cutting in line for the gas pump, vehicles in the background going the wrong way against traffic, and people walking in all directions. A first time visitor to Africa can experience sensory overload.

Moving through the less-than-systematized flow of vehicles and people, he began clicking away. After capturing all that humanity had to offer, he noticed the price of fuel and moved toward the street to get a good angle for the sign. Little did we know, there was a fuel pricing scandal happening within the country. Rumors of collusion, price gouging, and price-fixing were rampant in the media.

It was then that we found out we were being observed by another audience behind dark glass. A middle-aged Somali dressed in a neatly starched thobe came running out of the office. Finding the first anglo in the parking lot, he began to ask a long list of questions in broken English: Who are you? Where are you from? Where do you stay? Why are taking pictures of my gas pump?

Not getting many answers, he finally made his way to me. When I saw his furrowed brow and concerned look, I smiled big and said, "Asalaam wa aleikum."

The words stopped him in his tracks momentarily. Then he returned the proper greeting, "Aleikum salaam." Now that the tone of the conversation had been brought down three notches, he returned to his line of questions. "Why is he taking pictures of my gas station?"

"Very sorry, very sorry," I said in the local dialect. My understanding of the local language seemed to help his distress. "We are only here to wash our vehicle." I pointed to the 4X4 still parked in the washing bay.

"Where do you stay?" he asked with distrust.

"At the Somali Hotel," I said, motioning to the top of the building we could see from a block away. "In fact, the manager, Muhammad, is a good friend of mine. You can call him," I offered as I opened my phone to show him the number. Knowing how close-knit the community would be in that proximity gave me an opportunity to show we were part of the "in crowd."

Sliding into an opportunity to witness, I said, "We are followers of Isa al Masih, because of Al-Imran in Holy Qur'an. You know Al-Imran, right?"

The mention of a specific chapter often stuns the person listening and the usual nonverbal reaction followed my question. After a long pause, I happily filled in the silence.

"Al-Imran says the Masih Isa (PBUH) was born of a virgin named Maryam. This made Isa (PBUH) sinless and holy since he didn't inherit the problem started by the prophet Adam (PBUH). But then it says that he could heal the sick, and raise the dead. And when he was a small boy, he even breathed upon a clay bird and caused it to fly away."

I paused to receive any questions, objections, or comments. There were none. Instead, he turned and headed back to his office either because this Anglo-American quoting the Qur'an must have not been a threat or because the Somali was unwilling to continue a discussion about the theology that I was purportedly espousing.

Implications

In most Islamic cultures, relationship has a higher value than truth. Showing that you are not an outsider is very important to remain contextual. Without proof that I was an insider—or, more simply, that I was known by someone in the community—my actions and my entire entourage would have been suspect.

Secondly, defending my behavior from the Qur'an, albeit a very circular (nonlinear) argument for why my brother was taking photos, also showed that I held a value common to the people group. As the end result eventually bore out, he was not interested in spiritual truth about Jesus, yet my response from his book told him that I was not his enemy and I was not trying to adversely affect his business.

Circular arguments don't feel convincing to a linear-thinking Westerner. In fact, most struggle to connect how these type of arguments relate at all to the big picture.

Linear thinkers take pieces of truth and add them together to assemble a new and more complex thought. But in order to assimilate truths, there must be a consistent thread to connect them.

Circular thinkers don't need threads. They don't need progression. Their minds assimilate truth by extracting pieces of information that help them redesign an existing position rather than arrive at a conclusion or direction. These pieces of a big picture can be presented in any order and generally have to do with relationship more than fact.

As seen in dozens of training events, extremely few Westerners understand why a story of a clay bird being brought alive by Jesus is a compelling argument for non-Western Muslims. First, they oppose the story since it is not included in the Bible, and this omission sheds serious doubt on whether this particular miracle ever happened. Secondly, they argue that how it relates to Jesus's divine attributes is not readily apparent.

But before this story, in the presentation of Adam, we go a little out of the way to articulate how Adam was created. Putting forth the idea that Allah can breathe on clay to create humanity establishes a precedent. When we show that Jesus can create life in the same manner, we are putting him in the same category as God.

That type of argument seems to fail to accomplish the job as clearly as we would like because we, as Western thinkers, relate truths in a different manner. For a circular thinker to show or believe that both Allah and Jesus breathed life into clay means that Jesus is much more than a prophet.

Chapter 4
Find an Imam

Accompanying me on this trip were two friends who had asked several times in the preceding days, "When would I take them to a mosque?" We were in a war-torn Muslim country that was trying to recover and build its economy. Many mosques dotted the skyline, but I did not feel as though the right opportunity had presented itself.

We heard of a business fair in town and thought that a couple hours spent there would help us to gain knowledge about possibilities for new workers. We went and were given customized badges on lanyards and a bag full of advertisements and product samples.

Afterward, as we walked out into the warm evening air, I looked at my companions with their lanyards and their bags full of loot. It hit me that this was the moment; we were outfitted perfectly for stopping in a mosque. It would be obvious why we were in the city.

I hailed a cab. We hopped in. While pointing to a minaret on the horizon, I said to the driver, "Can you take us to that mosque?" My friends looked at me in unison and inquired, "Now?"

"Oh, yes," I replied. "This is the perfect opportunity."

We soon found ourselves in front of the mosque, and we told the taxi driver good-bye. He was a bit perplexed concerning why we hadn't asked him to wait. He could not understand what three Americans would do for an extended period in a mosque.

We watched our ride drive away and then stood looking at each other. I think my friends felt a little like the crew of the Spanish explorer Cortés, who told his men to burn the ships to keep them from sailing away. We were not on a main thoroughfare, and leaving in haste would not be possible.

They began removing their business fair name badges and were about to stash them in their bags when I corrected them. "No, no, no. Leave it all on, and bring it with you."

We entered the front of the mosque and removed our shoes at the door only to find a large crowd, perhaps forty people, walking toward us. Evening prayers had just finished. The whole group just stopped and stared.

I suppose the equivalent would be three men in checkered headdress with long white thobes walking through the front entrance of an evangelical church in America just as the Sunday morning service was being let out. The congregants emptying the pews would stop and stare, wondering what these men wanted.

I quickly greeted the crowd, "Asalaam wa aleikum," and waited for the response. Then I asked, "Does anyone here speak English?"

Two men in the back raised their hands up high and made their way to the front while repeating, "We do! We do!" Their excitement to help the new visitors was very apparent.

I asked if their imam was available. They quickly found his phone number and called him. He was still at his home and had not attended evening prayers. Once they had him on the line, he readily agreed to come and meet us.

We were ushered into his office where we were served juice, water, and crackers. Hospitality is always offered to visitors. The imam's office was nicely decorated with leather chairs, an executive desk, and a full wall of bookshelves. Our drinks were provided from a small fridge in the corner.

The imam arrived not too much later, and after introductions, I asked if my two newly acquired translators could help me tell a story. They readily agreed and leaned forward, eager to hear what I had to say. After all, it's not everyday that three American visitors stumble into a Middle Eastern mosque.

I began by saying that my favorite surah in the Holy Qur'an was Al-Imran. The translators, who were really structural engineers by day, forgot to translate because they were surprised I was quoting from the Qur'an. I politely asked if they could translate it into Arabic for the imam, and they bashfully turned back to the imam to update him.

My next statement was to explain that Isa al Masih (PBUH) was born to a virgin named Maryam and that the only other prophet without an earthly father was Adam. I paused again for my translators, who were still so enthralled they kept forgetting to translate. Once reminded, this time they seemed unwilling to come back to my story. They were quite satisfied to discuss the few new truths that I had raised.

I continued, "Adam (PBUH) was given life when Allah took clay from the ground and formed it into the shape of man. He breathed on the clay, and it came alive. Adam (PBUH) walked with Allah in paradise until something went very wrong. When things went very wrong, the children of Adam (PBUH) began fighting, even killing one another. The problem Adam (PBUH) started was passed not only to his children, but his grandchildren, and to their children. In fact, everyone in the line of Adam (PBUH) received the problem Adam (PBUH) started. All except one —Isa al Masih (PBUH), who had no earthly father. That makes Masih Isa (PBUH) sinless and holy."

It was a bit of a struggle to get my new engineer friends to translate that long story. With much urging and sometimes the need to interrupt a discussion that had broken out, we finally made it to the end.

Expecting to be able to continue, I was caught off guard when the imam asked a question in broken English. "I have question for you," he began. "Why is it in your holy book that we find prophets doing things that prophets would never do?" I waited patiently to see if he would provide an example so I could determine how much he knew of my holy book.

He continued stumbling to remember. "Why do we see the prophet Dau, Daudi, Dav?"

"David?" I gently interjected.

"Yes! David. Why do see him doing things with Batshe, Bathsa, Batsab?"

"Bathsheba," I said as I nodded knowingly.

"Yes, Bathsheba. Why do we see David doing things that a prophet would have never done?" His question was sincere and, amazingly, tied beautifully into the story I had just told.

"Very good question. Very good question," I responded. "I believe the answer lies in the story that began our discussion. After Adam (PBUH) ate of the forbidden fruit, he started a problem in the line of humanity that was visible in his children almost immediately. His children began killing, and at that time there was no previous killings. To answer your question, 'Why would David (PBUH) be found doing such things?' it is because he, too, was born in the line of Adam (PBUH). Everyone in the line of Adam inherited Adam's problem. All except one. Isa al Masih (PBUH) is the only one without the problem."

This answer triggered another discussion that went on for several minutes. It continued for so long between the imam and the translators that we three Americans sat back on the couch and began our own conversation with each other. After some time, the party of those sitting opposite us interrupted, having by then decided our session was drawing to a close. Both their nonverbal demeanor and their words of thanks signaled that we would now be leaving.

I took the opportunity to thank the imam repeatedly for his hospitality, his kindness, and the good discussion that I had greatly enjoyed. It was then that I remembered that a friend stateside had sent with me a hardbound, unabridged Arabic study Bible. I had packed it hoping it would be useful, since most of my conversations were with Muslims who were not ready to read another holy book.

"May I make a request of the imam?" I said.

"Like what kind of request?" the engineers responded with concern.

"I read and study Holy Qur'an. It would bless me greatly if in exchange for receiving an English translation of Qur'an, I could give him an Arabic translation of the Holy Bible."

My request was met with smiles and agreement. I was asked when we were leaving the country and when I would return to make the exchange. I let them know that my flight out of the country was the next day, but we would be certain to stop on the way to the airport.

We arrived at the mosque the next day and found the imam waiting for us. He was apologetic that he could not find an English Qur'an but readily received my gift and consented to a photo.

Implications

As much as I would have liked to complete the whole presentation, it is not possible to move someone in their understanding of Jesus beyond their willingness. Sensing when a person has reached his or her limit and letting up is very important, especially when working in shame-based cultures.

There are many worldview issues that must be introduced for a person to understand Jesus. Original sin, in this case, is a way of incriminating your audience while at the same time showing the unique nature of Christ. If the conversation had been allowed to continue, the same story of Adam would have been used to show that Adam (PBUH) could not overcome his single sin by obeying the five pillars of Islam. Instead, Allah had to cover Adam's sin with the skins of an animal. We call this "blood atonement."

The imam's question about David was highly significant. In a shame/honor culture, it is not appropriate to write about such sinful actions as the Bible does of the prophet David, even if they are known to be true. The stories in the Qur'an are largely whitewashed. Even Moses's act of killing an Egyptian is described literally as "to make an end of him." Prophets who sin are a problem theologically in Islam.

Knowing when to bring shame on the system and ultimately the person (when it is beneficial in helping them understand Jesus) and when to let go of something irrelevant to their salvation is wisdom only the Holy Spirit can provide. Westerners like to defend and correct all untruth, no matter how insignificant. To defend all truth, other than that which leads to knowing Christ, generally results in a dead end about an irrelevant issue.

There are numerous possible sidetracks that lead us away from the gospel in conversations with Muslims:

- the person of Muhammad
- prayer postures
- denominations
- the Crusades
- superiority of holy books
- which son, Ishmael or Isaac, was taken to be sacrificed (as described below)

I feel strongly these diversions should be viewed for what they really are: dead-end paths that veer away from the truth that leads to life. There is an appropriate time for such discussions. It is not necessary to agree with something that is not true; just overlook them at this juncture.

Until a person comes to faith in Jesus and receives the subsequent indwelling of the Holy Spirit (Eph. 1:13–14), a person has a limited capacity to comprehend spiritual truth. Only when a person is spiritually alive is discipleship or growth possible. We spend a large amount of time unnecessarily arguing with spiritually dead people about irrelevant truths.

Most Westernized believers are raised to tell "the truth, the whole truth, and nothing but the truth, so help me God."

That is a noble, cultural, and even Christian value which many other cultures have come to appreciate about America. However, when dealing with the vast amount of unbiblical information often encountered while dialoguing with a Muslim, attempting to correct every issue only leads to a divisive conversation.

One issue that I sidestep here is the debate over which son Abraham took up the mountain when his faith was tested. Genesis clearly states it was Isaac. Islam believes it was Ishmael, although the Qur'an does not ever say. It only says that he took "his son" after naming both of his sons just a few paragraphs before. It is inconclusive.

In reality, the answer is irrelevant for the salvific nature of the discussion at hand. It is not important which son was with Abraham. What is important is that God provided a substitute that had to be slaughtered in the son's place. Substitutionary atonement can clearly be pointed out in the story. Helping our Muslim friends understand that this atonement is the way God has always intended as the way of escape is paramount to getting them to Jesus.

Talking about ISA

Chapter 5
Make a "Close" Friend

Being in no particular hurry to meet my friend who was arriving at the immigration hall more than an hour after me, I strolled into the building and looked for a place to wait. A few rows of chairs in the corner opposite the visa counters were characteristically empty except for a man in a uniform with several stars on his shoulder.

 Though several chairs were empty, I chose the one immediately next to the man so that my elbow touched his. My own sense of personal space had been greatly diminished by living in East Africa for seven years. Touching people while sitting or passing in front of them so that our clothes brushed against each other was no longer too close. Even driving a vehicle inches from another without flinching was all too common.

After a long stillness of several minutes, longer than any Westerner normally would have allowed, I decided to break the silence. "I would sure like some chai. Do you know where I can get some chai?"

He lurched awake, rising from his chair so intent on honoring my request that he asked the South Asian man mopping the floor to get me a cup of chai. In surprise, the janitor looked at his mop bucket and shrugged, mumbling something about where am I supposed to get a cup of chai.

My new, starred-uniform friend reached out to me and said, "Come." We passed through the immigration counters where people were still lined up getting their visas, went down the hall to the right and into his personal office. I soon figured out that the man I had unwittingly befriended was the head of immigration for this particular Middle Eastern international airport.

After being seated in his office, he pulled an electric water kettle from below his desk and a bottle of water from his shelf. He poured the water into the kettle and heated it. Two unlikely potential friends then began getting to know one another. Although I was never asked what I did, the fact that I was en route to tour the Palestinian territory made a big impression.

As our small talk came to a close, I now held a cup of hot tea in my hand and asked him where he lived. Pulling out a large tourist map of his country from under the glass on his desk, he pointed to where he lived. To my delight, he lived within walking distance of a clearly marked tourist site labeled "The Baptism Site of Jesus."

I asked, "You live near the baptism site of Isa al Masih? That is really incredible. In fact my favorite surah in Holy Qur'an is about Masih Isa (PBUH). Is that a Qur'an behind you?" I asked, pointing to his bookshelf. He reached behind him to pull it down. By the stiffness of the pages as he opened the book, I surmised it was more of a decoration than anything else.

"Open to Al-Imran," I said excitedly. He searched long enough that it became readily apparent he did not know where it was. "The third surah, toward the front," I added. He switched directions and finally landed on it. "My favorite passage begins in aya 42," I said.

"It says that Masih Isa (PBUH) was born of a virgin named Maryam. Because he had no earthly father, that makes Isa sinless and holy. But it continues and says that Masih Isa (PBUH) could heal men born blind. Having no earthly father and the ability to heal the sick make Isa (PBUH) very, very special."

As I am reciting all of this, we are repeatedly interrupted from immigration workers needing paperwork signed by the immigration officer. Their reactions were remarkably similar: first, a surprised look that an American was in the office, and then, a second swift-eye glance at the Qur'an opened on their boss's desk. Then, as if nothing out of the ordinary was happening, the men return to the task at hand.

I continued with my presentation, "Isa (PBUH) could also raise the dead—by Allah's directive, of course. Isa did only what he saw Allah doing. But then it says that when Isa (PBUH) was a small boy, he took clay from the ground, formed it into the shape of a bird, and breathed on it, and it came alive and flew away."

My immigration friend, whose name I learned was Salaama, was both perplexed and uncomfortable at this point. He was willing to wade into a conversation about where he lived and even look up a passage in the Qur'an. But now he quickly changed the subject, unsure of what I would bring up next. I sensed his discomfort and left it there.

I told Salaama that my friend had probably arrived by now, and I should get my visa. He escorted me back to the visa line where I thanked him profusely for the chai and exchanged numbers so I could contact him in case I ever returned to his country, which I eventually did.

One Year Later

On arriving at the airport, I thought about the odds of Salaama still being in the same position. Knowing the way foreign governments move people to keep them from establishing a power center, I highly doubted it. But I needed to try. As I approached the immigration counter, I caught the eye of a supervisor and greeted him, "Asalaam wa aleikum."

"Aleikum salaam," he responded.

"Do you know Salaama?"

"Whose Salaama? Where?" he replied in a bit of confusion.

"Salaama is *habibi*," I said pointing to my shoulder with three fingers extended to simulate the stars of his rank. I continued, "Salaama is my friend. Office that way," extending my arm toward the hallway that I had walked a year before.

"One minute," he replied, holding up a finger and then quickly disappearing down a different hallway.

I finished paying for my visa and getting my passport stamped. After clearing the barrier, I decided to wait a few minutes—or at least until another immigration officer questioned me or motioned me to move on to the luggage hall.

Soon the supervisor returned from the same hallway he had gone down and motioned for me to follow him. He led me into another office with three desks, all of them occupied by lower ranking officials than Salaama, at least by my guess according to their lack of stars.

"This is Salaama's cousin," he said introducing me to one of the individuals.

"*Alhumdulilah*," I said excitedly. "Where is Salaama?"

"He transferred, city far away," came his cousin's response. "You like talk to Salaama now?" his cousin asked in broken English, showing me his cell phone.

"*Aywa. Aywa!*" I exclaimed.

He dialed Salaama's number and spoke for few seconds in Arabic, and then in broken English he said, "Here? At airport? One minute, one minute. You talk to him." He handed me the phone.

"Asalaam wa aleikum!" I began.

"Aleikum salaam," he returned and then added. "I'm here at the airport. I would like to see you."

Phone conversations about details with someone whose first language is different from yours is nearly always pointless. "I'm coming. I'm coming. Two minutes," I responded, assuming he would be in the international arrival area. I returned the phone to his cousin who I was sure would sort out the details.

I thanked the man who had led me to Salaama's cousin and left to make my way downstairs to the luggage hall. As I stepped on the escalator, there was Salaama at the bottom, waiting for me with two other friends.

"*Masha'allah*," I announced, and I gave him a hug, touching his cheeks on both sides with my cheek. I could not believe that though he had been transferred to manage another port of entry, God had arranged for him to be at the airport picking up guests the same day and time I arrived.

After exchanging greetings, he began to inquire about my schedule. I again was heading to a Palestinian-controlled territory, but this time I had failed to plan for the border closing. It closed every Saturday at noon, and it was already past that time.

So Salaama said, "No problem, James. You must stay at my house tonight. No problem. No problem. My brother is crossing the border in the morning when it opens. He can drive you there. You just come. No problem. No problem. You will be our guest."

How could I refuse an offer like that? Even better, it gave me opportunity to once again raise the importance of the qurban of Isa. We piled into his car, made the long drive down to his home, ate dinner at his home, and then spent the night there. There can be no better opportunity to win trust than to spend the night at a Muslim family's home.

On our thirty minute drive to his house, I realized that after I had exited the plane and excitedly pursued finding Salaama, I had failed to stop at a bathroom. Arriving near the point of pain, I was going to have to interrupt our drive with a bathroom break. Rarely are public bathrooms readily available, even in a city. Most of those in restaurants are only available for customers. Having lived in East Africa for a number of years, I was more than prepared to use a tree, a ditch, or step out behind a building.

After interrupting my host with my urgent need, we conveniently came upon a mosque, the only one we had seen on our drive. If there is one place that would always have a bathroom, it is a mosque. We stopped. I opened the car door to run inside, and at that very moment, the call to prayer began from the megaphone on top of the minaret. Incredible timing, I thought. You just can't plan this stuff.

After learning where the bathroom was, I went inside to the left, where a few Muslim men were performing ablution, the purification washing needed before prayers. As I glanced over to the main door, Salaama and his friends were walking straight into the prayer hall. The three men were convicted by being in the presence of a visitor and wanted to show that they were practicing their faith. I doubt we would have stopped had I not needed to use the facilities. They had all reluctantly piled out of the car and headed inside for prayers.

After a few quick splashes of water on face, I left the bathroom and made my way back to the entrance. Prayers were just beginning. Without hesitation I removed my shoes and took a position in the prayer line next to my three car companions. I participated in the prayer postures while praying in my heart that Jesus would open their eyes to him. The short, seven-minute service ended, and as usual, all the men who had been praying left abruptly to return to their day. We made our way back outside to the car to continue to Salaama's house.

Since the car was filled with Arabic, I looked out the window at the passing barren landscape. I occasionally would glance into Salaama's eyes in the car's rearview mirror and smile. One of those looks spawned a conversation.

"James!" he said quizzically. "Are you a Muslim?" It's a question I am accustomed to getting and one that I eagerly invite. Anytime you pray in the postures of a Muslim, use a few Arabic words, or quote from the Qur'an, you will get the question.

"You will remember from last year, Salaama, I'm a follower of Isa al Masih (PBUH), because of the third surah, Al-Imran." His forehead furrowed slightly, and he did not pursue the matter further. I was hopeful that once his other friends had been dropped off, he would be open to a deeper conversation. He never brought it up again the rest of the evening, nor the next morning. So neither did I.

Implications

A person of peace is an individual who responds in a positive way to spiritual truth. This can be in words, body language, or even neutral feedback. The only way to know a person who is not firmly against what you are saying is to push ahead assuming they are in agreement.

Once a person has been exposed to truth twice, and they show no interest or make it perfectly clear they have no use for what you are sharing, shake the dust off your feet and move on. God has someone else prepared for you to talk about Jesus with.

Of course this doesn't mean I block them on Facebook and refuse text messages. I have many friends who are not persons of peace. What it does mean is that they do not receive the prioritized time that a person who continues to respond positively would get. Some are just not ready yet.

We should not see a lack of interest in the gospel as a defeat, but see it as God redirecting you to someone who is ready to hear. The only way a gospel presentation is a failure on our part is if we fail to communicate it in a way that can be understood. It is a hard thing to hear, but if we

Talking about ISA

are presenting Jesus to another culture in a way that makes good sense to us, is emotionally moving to our hearts, and causes our spirit to rejoice, we are probably not communicating cross-culturally.

Let me illustrate from another world religion's vantage point. To a Westernized evangelical, John 3:16 is the preeminent passage to illustrate their faith. It is often quoted to many cross-cultural audiences, including Buddhists. We know it well:

For God so loved the world, that He gave His only begotten Son, that whosoever shall believe in Him, should not perish but have everlasting life.

—John 3:16, NASB

That truth seems straightforward. And it is, if you were raised with a Judeo-Christian worldview and know how to define the terms. Someone from a Buddhist background defines the terms very differently. How might John 3:16 sound to a Buddhist? His thoughts are in parenthesis below:

For God... (*Well, there is no god. God is everything and in everything.*) ...so loved... (*Love? Doesn't this god know that we must let go of every emotion in order to be set free from pain? This god is not very far on the path to nirvana.*) ...the world... (*God is in everything, including the world. This god must love himself.*) ...that He gave his only begotten son... (*A god who has children, how absurd!*) ...that whoever believes in Him... (*Believe is all that's required? What a weak system. Everyone knows you must strive diligently our entire lives to escape this cycle of reincarnation. Plus, you can only depend on yourself. Never on anyone else.*) ...shall not perish,... (*Perish? Perish isn't an option. No one perishes. If we fail we are reincarnated*) ...but have everlasting life. (*That sounds terrible. Life is suffering. To continue to live forever is the worst hell I can imagine. No thank you. I don't want this religion, or this god, or his son.*)

Here is John 3:16, rewritten the way a Buddhist world view would interpret it:

> *Everything that exists failed to empty itself of emotion to escape pain and instead loved itself. It gave birth to a son and requires the weakest of responses, mere belief, instead of dedication and learning to avoid perishing, which isn't a possibility anyway. The end result is that you are trapped in a life of pain, never to escape.*

If we have made every attempt possible to make the person of Christ and his work on our behalf clear, and the person rejects our message, we should feel successful at being obedient. They are not rejecting us; they are rejecting Jesus. Jesus warned us that if they didn't like him, they would not like us since we carry his message of salvation.

Very often, adopting a few culturally appropriate behaviors helps open the ears of our listeners, but never the behaviors that are clearly sin, such as praying to idols, using charms, or denying Christ. That would be counterproductive.

In Acts 21:26, we find that Paul, a Jew, offered sacrifices in the temple at the conclusion of his ministry before appealing to Caesar. He never trusted those sacrifices to make him clean in God's eyes. His argues throughout his letters that keeping the law is of no use. But he did strive to be viewed as clean in the culture's eyes. He viewed this as a helpful step in gaining a hearing for his faith in Christ.

Praying in a prostrated position can be an emotionally charged subject. Many debate on whether or not a follower of Jesus should enter a mosque and participate in prayers. It was helpful for me to have an understanding of what the postures meant before I committed to doing them.

The first is hands cupped behind your ears. It means I am here to listen to what God has to say. The second is left hand over the belt, right hand over the left hand, to reflect the idea that I am here to receive fullness from him.

The beginning of prostrating yourself is to bow. Bowing and placing your hands on your knees, shows that you are submissive to the will of God. Then finally, Muslims bend their knees to the ground, place their hands ahead of them and put their head on the ground. This is the ultimate position of submission.

All of these concepts are repeated in the Old Testament. In fact, the term for prostrate or bow is used 165 times. One of those occurrences happens in the context of a Gentile from Assyria who came to know the God of Israel. But because of his job, he had to bow in the House of Rimmon. Naaman asks special forgiveness from Elisha for bowing to a pagan altar:

"In this matter may the Lord pardon your servant: when my master goes into the house of Rimmon to worship there, and he leans on my hand and I bow myself in the house of Rimmon, when I bow myself in the house of Rimmon, the Lord pardon your servant in this matter." He (Elisha) said to him, "Go in peace."

— *2 Kings 5:18–19, NASB*

Elisha's response to a new follower of *Yehova* is striking. No one in the postresurrection period of our faith would advocate going into a Hindu temple and bowing before an idol. Elisha's grace extended to this sincere request should remind us that while man looks on the outside, God looks at the heart.

To be clear, I'm not comparing this very unique, idolatrous temple in 2 Kings to a mosque. They are quite different. For a monotheistic religion like Islam, which forbids any visible idol or image in their mosque, it would be very appropriate to offer prayers to the God of Abraham, Noah, Moses, David, Jonah, and John the Baptist, all of whom are mentioned in the Qur'an. Our presence in such a place gives us the ability to clarify bad theology.

Chapter 6
No Room at the Inn

Having become accustomed to lodging in a room at the Somali hotel whenever I visited this capital city, I soon stopped texting ahead to make a reservation. It was one of these times that landed me in the best position possible for sharing Jesus.

I arrived on an evening flight and made my way after dark to the hotel to check in. I told the taxi to wait for me while I ran inside to secure my room since I planned to go out for dinner. At the hotel's front desk, I learned that a Muslim delegation from Sudan was in town and had taken all the rooms.

"What should I do?" I asked my friend at the desk, with whom I was, by then, on a first name basis.

"No problem, no problem. I have another place not far," he answered. I could not think of another hotel in the area, so I ventured to ask for more information.

"You run two hotels?" I queried in amazement.

"No, not a hotel," came the reply. "It's a guesthouse. Very private. Very safe. I'll take you there. Just give me a few minutes to arrange."

I went back outside to my taxi to tell the driver that my needs were taken care of, even though I didn't know where I would be going or how long it would take me to get there. The taxi driver and I had also developed a relationship over time, and he liked to look out for my well being as well. His quizzical expression confirmed that it was with good reason that I had already been questioning my decision. However, I said goodbye to him and waited on the sidewalk with my two bags for the hotel manager.

Soon he appeared at the doorway to the hotel with his phone at his ear while searching the streets for what I assumed would be my car to the guesthouse. A small Toyota pulled up in front of me. The manager reached the curb and opened the back door for me while the driver jumped out to put my bags in the trunk.

Definitely good customer service, but customer service to where?

We were soon heading down a side street lined with small houses. We pulled up in front of one that looked liked all of the others except for a plywood sign in Arabic next to the second-story window.

On entering, I met Adam, who was in his mid twenties and introduced himself as the guesthouse manager. I was delighted at his name because it made an easy bridge to my story about the first qurban, which Allah provided for Adam. He took me to the second floor and opened the door to a very spacious and nicely kept bedroom with a queen-size bed. The bathroom was clean and stocked with tissue, towels, soap, and a shower curtain, which was a bit uncommon for this part of the country.

I arranged my things and contemplated going straight to sleep since it was already past ten o'clock at night. I kept thinking of Adam, sitting by himself downstairs, and how I would like for him to hear the story then. Who knew what distractions might await me in the morning before my taxi picked me up? So I went back downstairs to where I expected him to be.

I greeted him for the second time. "Asalaam wa aleikum!"

"Hello and good evening!" came his reply. I always chuckle at the response of people around the world who are as eager to greet Westerners in their appropriate way as those of us Westerners who work hard at contextualization for the cultures we visit.

"I'm a little hungry. Want to walk over to the hotel and see if they have anything to eat?" I asked. Being very inclined to escape a post that had no activity, he accepted immediately. Soon we were walking down the darkened street back toward the hotel that I had just left.

"What was your name again?" I asked innocently.

"Adam," he said.

"Masha'allah." I said. "Adam (PBUH) was the first prophet. And you know how he was created? He didn't have an earthly father. It was the *Ruah Allah* that caused the clay in paradise to come alive."

He chimed in. "Yes, you are correct, and did you know that Moses was actually not a man, but instead he was the angel Gabriel."

I was shocked at the statement and tried hard not to take the bait and get pulled off track. Many stories—most of them very illogical and even absurd—often come out at a time like this. Engaging them and even trying to address all of the problems in a story is a pointless venture.

"I did not know that," I replied. "You are the first one to tell me this. However, you do know what happened to Adam (PBUH) in paradise not long after Allah breathed life into him?"

"Oh yes, I learned this in *madrasa*. Adam (PBUH) ate of the forbidden fruit," he said, recalling elementary school.

"Exactly, and that one sin caused Allah to remove him from paradise. Just one sin and Adam (PBUH) could not walk with Allah or even be in his presence. But you know what Allah did? He made Adam clothes. He performed qurban on an animal and covered Adam's sin and shame with the skin. This is how Allah has always dealt with sin and shame."

Completely avoiding my new revealed concept, my friend returned to his story about Moses, this time with more detail about *jinn* (genies), angels, and Gabriel. This talk took us all the way back to the hotel. Any spiritual breakthrough was indeterminable. The concept of sin and shame and overcoming it had held no consequence for this Adam. I decided at this point not to return to the story.

After a very nicely prepared meal at the Somali hotel, we returned to the guesthouse. Before closing my eyes, I grabbed my phone, searched for the morning prayer time in that country, and set my alarm. I drifted off to sleep imagining how surprised Adam would be when I showed up a few minutes before early morning prayers, ready to pray with him.

There was no need to wait for my 5:26 a.m. alarm to go off. I was wide awake at 4:00 a.m. already. I had tossed and turned, wide awake from the effects of jet lag. Not wanting to get back in my travel clothes but wanting to see who was downstairs getting ready for prayers, I walked down the flights of stairs in the soccer shorts and t-shirt I had slept in.

Upon reaching the foyer, I noticed it was deadly quiet. No noise, no stirring, and no prayers. I gently pushed open one of the double doors leading to the family room, thinking I could wait around for someone to present themselves. I was shocked to see the floor full of Somalis on foam mattresses.

The light from the foyer reflecting into the room revealed at least five men in their Muslim attire lying asleep. Nearest the door and getting the brunt of the light, a young man rolled over to look at who was disturbing him.

In response, all I knew to say was "*Salaat?*" while pointing at my watch.

He rolled back over and pushed a button on his cell phone to illuminate its face and then began mumbling to everyone, "Salaat, salaat, salaat." Soon the lights were on and everyone was moving their mattresses to the side of the room. I joined the line-up that had now formed and was preparing to begin the prayer postures when, one-by-one, my new friends leaned over to look down at my exposed knees. I had forgotten I was still in soccer shorts. Definitely a no-no for prayers.

"Can you go to your room and find a towel or sheet to cover yourself appropriately?" they requested.

I quickly obliged and soon was joining them dressed like a fraternity party participant in a toga. We continued with prayers, first holding our hands behind our ears, then bowing with our hands on our knees, followed by full prostration on our knees with our foreheads to the ground. After two full cycles, we now ended on our bottoms with our feet tucked to one side.

The older gentleman, whom I assumed was an elder in the group, slowly crawled forward and then made a semi-circle to come face-to-face with me. With a Somali now on both of sides of me and the ringleader sitting square in front of me, I was very curious where this was going.

"Are you a Muslim?" he asked in crystal-clear English.

"Actually, I'm a follower of Isa al Masih, (PBUH)."

His wrinkled brow told me that he needed a bit more information. I added, "I follow the qurban of Isa because of Al-Imran in the Holy Qur'an. Do you have a Qur'an? I can show you."

A quick glance around the room turned up no Qur'an, and so I continued my explanation. "It says beginning in aya 42 that Isa al Masih (PBUH) was born of a virgin named Maryam. Why is this important? In order to understand, we have to look at the only other prophet who didn't have an earthly father, Adam (PBUH).

"Adam (PBUH) was created in paradise when Allah took clay from the ground, fashioned it into the shape of a man, and then breathed life into him. He walked with Allah until something happened. When that event happened, the children of Adam (PBUH) began killing one another. The problem not only passed to the children but to the grandchildren and the great grandchildren.

"In fact, all of the children of Adam (PBUH) inherited the problem that he started, and the children of Adam

(PBUH) are still killing each other to this today. That is, all except one man in the line of Adam (PBUH). There is only one who was sinless and holy. There is only one who was born of a woman and had no earthly father: Isa al Masih (PBUH)."

A slight pause to look around the room revealed intent eyes and ears. No one was upset, and my audience of five did not blink nor offer a rebuttal. It was about 5:50 a.m., and I knew my taxi had planned to pick me up at 6:00. I needed to keep moving, or I would run out of time to catch my in-country flight.

"Isa is sinless and holy, the scripture continues to say, and it also says that Masih Isa (PBUH) could heal the man who was born blind. He is the only prophet who could do this. Then the third surah says Masih Isa (PBUH) could raise the dead.

"When Isa was a small boy, the Holy Qur'an says that Isa took clay from the ground and fashioned it into the shape of bird. He breathed on it, and it came alive and flew away. Masih Isa could create life.

"All those things are important, but the most important reason that I follow Isa (PBUH) is because of aya 55 in Al-Imran. It says that Allah *mutawafeeka* Isa. And you know what *mutawafeeka* means? It comes from the root word *wafat,* which means to kill. Allah offered his blameless Holy Lamb, Masih Isa, as a qurban to remove our sin and shame."

Then as if someone had planned the preceding events with precision, my phone lying in front of me began to ring. I looked down at the number. I let my audience know that my taxi was waiting outside to take me to the airport.

I stood to my feet and turned to go back upstairs to pack. In an attempt to stop me, the elder of the Somalis replied, "Wait just a minute. You can't go yet. What did you say your name was?"

"Bryanson," I responded. "It's Scottish. From Scotland," I said, adding the tag in hopes that the name would be more acceptable.

"From now on," the elder added, "we will call you Ibrahim because you are a man of great faith. We have never seen anyone with such great faith who would wake us up for morning prayers."

I gathered my things and headed outside, still marveling at what had just happened.

Implications

When Jesus sent his disciples out in Luke 10 to begin ministry in area villages, he sent them out under orders not to take an extra coat or pair of shoes. What is more telling is that they weren't allowed to take money either. It's a seemingly difficult passage in light of modern day efforts to attract followers through a variety of services, goods, and food.

It seems that Jesus was wanting to put his followers in a position of humility rather than a position of power. Not only humble, they were vulnerable. Their needs for that day as well as overnight lodging were dependent on the reception of their message.

I obviously was a paying customer in this story. But putting myself with no protection in a guesthouse of Somalis and in a position at their complete mercy was a position of humility. The reverse effect, of me being at their mercy, put them at complete ease. Even better, when I demonstrated by my actions that I was not opposed to their culture, it allowed them to let down their guard even more.

The term *Christian* has unfortunately lost its meaning in our world today. In the recent era, Christians in Hitler's Germany, the Rwandan Hutus, and the Maronites in Lebanon all committed atrocities that other religions are quick to point out as part of the Christian legacy. Yes, I am aware of the atrocities committed by those of the Muslim faith, but we have to remember that all cultures are much quicker to point out others' faults than their own.

As if the lost meaning of *Christian* as a "follower of Christ" were not enough, a mentality that the United States comprises only Christians pervades the Muslim world. Hollywood exports a variety of the world's vices that are interpreted as being Christian practices. Women who reveal way too much skin, prolific alcohol use, and visible idols in religion are just a few.

Most Muslims associate the Christian faith with polytheism. In their belief system, there can be no pictures of prophets. Also, statues, stained glass, or jewelry that depicts Jesus, Muhammad, or any of the other Old Testament messengers are completely forbidden.

When you are in a Muslim culture, calling yourself a Christian creates an ambiguity. Who and what are you really representing? Is yours just another religion that requires performing a different set of actions to get God's favor? Even in the West, there is a growing need to identify with being a "follower of Jesus" to distinguish our beliefs from the world religion called "Christianity" that has often been mistaken for our true faith.

The idea of "conversion to Christianity" is no longer what it originally meant. It traditionally meant that someone stopped following their path of good works or allegiance to a false god and now has chosen to receive what Jesus did in making a pathway to God. You will note in the dialogue, I was not interested in converting these Somalis to Christianity; I was interested in telling them about Jesus.

Equally important to remember is that singing songs, whether hymns or praise choruses, is not a part of Islamic worship. Muslims do not sing together. They recite verses in a melodious chant and bow in a group as a symbol of unity of purpose and strength with their fellow brothers.

Talking about ISA

Chapter 7
Island Hopping

It's always exhilarating to arrive at a major African airport with nine Americans on their first visit. Watching someone experience the sights, smells, and humanity followed by a litany of questions is even more fun. Everyone was quite astonished to learn a few days later that there had been a hand grenade attack the very afternoon we had landed in that city.

On arriving at our coastal guesthouse, the majority on the trip were pleasantly surprised at the accommodations. Thatched roofs from palm fronds, showers, Western toilets, and even hot water were unexpected in this developing country. The fresh seafood offered for the evening meals added even more to their delight.

Teams of four spent several days in the local markets, beaches, and shops. They had a great time fishing for men, discovering several persons of peace. A few team members were even more adventurous than others. They discovered and embarked on a *dhow* cruise, an East African sailboat that sailed to a nearby island for a seafood dinner. This *dhow* regularly stopped at a marine park that featured excellent snorkeling on the way back.

After enjoying a meal on the island, several were eager to return the next day. Except this next time, they wanted to be bolder in sharing about Isa and not just enjoying the day's catch. Three of us drove to the dock the next morning to catch the *dhow*. As it made its way across the channel, we soon found ourselves watching dolphins dance in the waves off the bow.

We were quickly mistaken for tourists. Not a bad thing, I thought. What better way to be taken in and introduced to people with whom we would like to share Isa.

On the island, after a short walk up a rocky path, we reached the edge of a short cliff with a single, covered row of seats facing the aqua lagoon where the *dhow* that had carried us now sat gently bobbing in the crystal-clear waters.

Before long, we were dining on a big meal of freshly caught seafood. First a whole crab, then a grilled sea bass, followed by a whole lobster, shrimp, and finally mussels. We were overwhelmed with food and felt we had truly discovered paradise. The cool breeze coming off the water was enough to make anyone consider relocating. The view alone gave one pause concerning preconceived retirement plans. Then our senses turned back to reality, and we refocused on our intended task.

Instead of making our way back down the trail toward the lagoon as most tourists would, I led our small party away from the water down a path that only locals trekked. The island was known to have held a Muslim community for many centuries, and few, if any, Christians had ever ventured out to share with them.

We first encountered children moving along the pathways. Soon after, we began to encounter rudimentary shelters. Some had windows and others had none. Some were built of local palm fronds and wood. Others were made from blocks cut from a quarry of long-dead coral.

We greeted people with the traditional "Asalaam wa aleikum" and continued along the path. We could tell the trail was beginning to circle back toward the water and soon came across a large meeting area, an open-air hut where many of the men had gathered to play checkers, discuss politics, and enjoy the cool breeze.

Our anglo party made its way down to the gathering, seemingly unnoticed. I took an empty seat on a bench while my two prayer warriors stayed on the perimeter. I opted to make no attempt to introduce myself or interrupt the ongoing social interactions. Within a few minutes, a man who must have been a leader in the group turned to me and said, "Tell us something." I took that as a cue for my story from the Qur'an.

"I'm a follower of Isa al Masih (PBUH)," I said. "I follow Masih Isa because of Al-Imran in Holy Qur'an. Beginning in aya 42, it says that Masih Isa was born of a virgin named Maryam. This is very important because there was only one other prophet that did not have an earthly father: Adam (PBUH). This first prophet was made when Allah took clay from the ground, fashioned it into the shape of man and breathed on it—the Ruah Allah—and Adam (PBUH) came alive."

I looked around the group as I was talking. About one-third went on with their conversations, another third were listening, and the other third pretended they were not listening though I soon found out that they were following the conversation. In a gathering of Muslims, it is not always publicly acceptable to listen to someone talking about Jesus. Since there was no response to my opening introduction, I just continued.

"Adam (PBUH) walked with Allah in paradise until something went very wrong. When that happened, his children began killing one another. In fact, the problem that he gave to his children was passed on to their children, and then to the grandchildren. Everyone in the line of Adam (PBUH) inherited the problem he started. Everyone except one: Masih Isa. That makes Isa sinless and holy. He did not have an earthly father, and so, he did not inherit the problem Adam (PBUH) started."

When I took a slight breath and looked up, the number still making eye contact was down to three. I had become so focused on my story that I had not noticed a young man with a beard and white thobe—the only one wearing a thobe—come into the group.

I continued, "Masih Isa (PBUH) is not only sinless and holy, but it then says in surah Al-Imran that Masih Isa (PBUH) had the power to heal the sick. There was a man who was born blind, and Masih Isa (PBUH) enabled him to see. It then says that Masih Isa (PBUH) was able to raise the dead. These two signs make Masih Isa very special and very different from the other prophets."

At this point, the young man in the thobe apparently had heard enough of my teaching from the Qur'an. Although I had not yet said anything contradictory to Islamic theology, he wasn't going to let a Westerner sit and teach his people. I can only assume that he felt his turf had been invaded.

I was not entirely certain of his agenda, but I could tell by his raised voice, wrinkled brow, and his repeated mention of the name Isa (ironically, without the required PBUH) that he was trying to downgrade Jesus after I had lifted him up.

I sat there listening intently at his rant. I did not offer any argument in response. Instead, the others in the group stood up and began arguing with him. I was pleasantly surprised that others had valued my Qur'an lesson, and was delighted that they had come to my rescue.

However, it soon became evident that it was more of an argument than a discussion. I stood momentarily to see if I would be addressed. I was not. So I turned to one of the bystanders and said, "Sorry, but we should probably head back to our resort now."

We slowly made our way back down the path to the lagoon where we boarded the small row boat to be taken back to the *dhow*. Upon boarding the *dhow*, we set sail for the mainland and looked back to the island to see what had happened to our gathering. A crowd larger than the one we had left had assembled, and we may never know the outcome of their discussion about the uniqueness of this man called "Jesus the Messiah."

Implications

One of the failures of this trip, and of my early incursions into Islamic areas to raise up Jesus, was my lack of preparedness to leave bread crumbs. As in the story of Hansel and Gretel, these morsels of substance were a means for getting back to the source. The difference in this case is that you leave behind these crumbs so that the person of peace can find you later.

These bread crumbs can be a business card from the reception desk of your hotel, which would get them to your location but not compromise your room number. They can also be a simple preprinted business card with a dedicated prepaid phone number or dedicated e-mail address that you use only for outreach.

Whatever the case, if one or more Muslims hear your story of Jesus and want to know more, they need to have a way to get in touch with you again. Perhaps it won't be that very night. It might be in the future after they have a dream or vision of a man in a brilliant white robe appearing to them. At that time, they will surely want to know more.

This scenario on the island, or one like it, can also serve as the most powerful training class that you can offer others. When someone goes with you and sees your boldness in a public setting, it emboldens them as well. It has often been said that your disciple will never be more bold than what he observes in your actions. That may be a bit overstated for effect, but in reality, people don't do what they hear others saying; they do what they see others doing.

Chapter 8
Refugee Camp Reprieve

My third visit to a refugee camp of course didn't give me as much confidence for understanding the local people group as those who had lived among them for years, yet I had enough confidence by then that I decided it was time to venture out.

My wife Tamar was traveling with me, along with three others, and we joined an interesting sounding tour of the greenhouse-like gardens that had been constructed in different areas of the refugee community. An industrious, forward-thinking national named Baasit was our tour guide.

Baasit was liked by most who knew him. He had a knack for overcoming obstacles and figuring out complex agriculture solutions that had never been encountered in his region. He also had a reputation for something else: being shut off to the gospel. It is uncertain what he had heard, who had shared, or why he was resistant, but the reputation had stuck—Baasit was closed to the gospel.

We ventured out in his car and stopped several times at different greenhouses. I became impressed after seeing several gardens with produce of lettuce, tomatoes, onions, and eggplants. As we viewed one especially large garden, the owner came out of her house to greet us.

We were on a limited schedule and had planned to leave for the next site a few minutes later. But to to have a more fruitful conversation with the woman—and allow my friends traveling with me to experience it—we needed to be invited inside a home.

After asking Baasit to translate a brief conversation with the woman, I pointed out how beautiful I thought the henna was on her hand. The compliment pleased her. She invited us in for tea, offering to decorate my wife's hand. Tamar willingly agreed.

The tea ceremony alone was a fairly long and drawn out event. A charcoal stove had to be prepped and lit. A young man in the family fanned the coals for several minutes until they were hot enough to heat water in a kettle. When the tea was ready, the woman began a long pouring ceremony to create foam. This happens by lifting a glass about two feet above another. The pouring back and forth between glasses creates enough foam to make them look full.

After preparing the tea, the woman and her sister prepped the henna root powder, which was another long endeavor. When it was ready, the sister started to paint a design on Tamar's hand.

All of this was exactly what I greatly desired. Getting into an intimate setting where a prolonged presence gives enough time for people to feel comfortable was the goal. On most tours, this side distraction would have completely interrupted the schedule of the day; for our purposes, this side tour *was* our intended schedule. We were nestled on large floor cushions with both activities well under way when I noticed that Baasit was no longer with us.

He was pretty important. Not only was he well respected and the catalyst in helping start the gardens, but he was also the only fluent English speaker who could translate into the local dialect.

The first cup of tea had long been made and drunk before he showed up again. I had almost began to think that our social gathering had been in vain. Tamar was well over halfway into her henna treatment when Baasit walked in.

He made small talk in the local dialect and then took a position across the room from me, sitting on a cushion.

After a few moments of allowing the atmosphere to settle, I asked Baasit if he would be willing to translate to the group a story from the Holy Qur'an. He obliged without giving it a second thought.

"My story about the straight path to paradise begins in the third surah of the Holy Qur'an, Al-Imran," I said, as usual. "It says that the virgin Maryam gave birth to a son who was named Isa al Masih (PBUH). Masih Isa (PBUH) had no earthly father. That made him very special. The only other prophet who did not have an earthly father, was the first prophet, Adam (PBUH).

"Adam (PBUH) was created when Allah breathed on clay that he had formed into the shape of man. Adam walked with Allah in paradise until something went very wrong. The children of Adam (PBUH) began killing one another. In fact, the problem they inherited from their father was passed to their children, and even on to their grandchildren. In fact every child in the line of Adam (PBUH) all the way up until now received the problem that he started. All of them except one. There is one in the line of Adam that did not have the problem passed down to him through bloodline: that is Isa al Masih. And that makes Masih Isa (PBUH) sinless and holy, the only sinless one in the line of Adam (PBUH)."

I finished the first part of the story, and while the last few lines were being translated, I picked up my tea glass and finished drinking its contents. I turned and looked inquisitively at the young man in front of the charcoal as if to say, "Any left?" He reached for my empty glass and began filling it. As he did so, I turned and looked at Tamar and asked her how the henna was going. By this point, the tips of her fingers were covered in balls of a moist paste, and the rest of her hands were decorated in a brown pattern.

During this time, I made sure not to make eye contact with Baasit. I had spoken very prominently of Jesus in a room full of Muslims, and I needed his permission to continue. He was putting himself on the line by being the translator, and I did not want him to feel forced or pressured.

Now with a newly filled glass of tea, I took a sip. Feeling his eyes return to me, I looked up to see his raised eyebrow signaling for me to keep going. So I did.

"Isa al Masih (PBUH) is not only sinless and holy, but Al-Imran tells us that he had the power to heal the sick. He touched a man who had been blind since birth and now the man was able to see. It also says in aya 49 that Masih Isa could raise the dead. Of course this was at Allah's permission. It continues and says that when Masih Isa (PBUH) was a small boy, he took clay from the ground and fashioned it into the shape of bird. He breathed on the clay, and the bird came to life and took flight. Isa al Masih (PBUH) could also create life.

"Being the only one in the line of Adam (PBUH) without an earthly father makes him sinless and holy. The ability to heal the sick, raise the dead, and create life, make him very special—different than anyone else who has walked on earth."

I had traveled through enough material by this point that it would be very obvious where I was going. I would need to be very cautious and use wisdom if I were to continue speaking. If Baasit gave a very hesitant or dismissive signal, I would need to wrap it up and end the story.

I once again picked up my tea and waited patiently. I watched with a smile as the ladies sat with their outstretched hands, covered in henna, waiting for them to dry. The room sat very silent, almost anticipating the great climax of my story. I once again felt Bassit's eyes on my face. I turned and received a nod of approval to continue.

With great eagerness and conviction, I pressed on. "All of these things about Isa (PBUH) make him very, very special. However, aya 55 in the third surah is the most important truth to realize. What Holy Qur'an says is 'Allah mutawafeeka Isa.' The word *mutwafeeka* comes from *wafat*, meaning to die. Qur'an says it was Allah who offered Isa as a qurban. This is important because this is how Allah removes sin and shame, through qurban.

"The first qurban was offered for Adam and *Hawwa* (Eve) when they were removed from paradise for only one sin. One sin—eating the forbidden fruit—and the first prophet could no longer be with Allah in paradise. Adam tried to cover his sin and shame by weaving leaves for clothes. But Allah said in surah 7 that he must make the clothes. He slaughtered a lamb and took the skin and covered their sin and their shame. This was the first qurban.

"The second qurban was provided for Ibrahim when he took his son up the mountain. We all know that Allah stopped Ibrahim from sacrificing his son. It was a test of faith that he passed beautifully. Allah stopped Ibrahim and said, 'Look, there in the bushes I have provided a substitute qurban for your son.' Allah can provide something to die in place of someone else. Allah can provide a substitute qurban so that someone else may live.

"There is one more qurban that Allah performed himself. It is the greatest because it has the ability to remove all sin and shame from you and me. It is what I have just shown you in aya 55 of Al-Imran: 'Allah mutwafeeka Isa.' This is when Allah sacrificed his blameless Holy Lamb, Isa al Masih, as the last and greatest qurban. He then raised Isa from the dead, and Isa traveled a straight path to paradise where he is now waiting to come back. If you receive the qurban of Masih Isa, you can have your sins and shame removed and be guaranteed a place in paradise."

Baasit finished the translating, and I looked around the room to find ten smiling faces. My eyes met Baasit's. They were filled with a look of appreciation and care. Then he quickly jumped to his feet and told us we were very late and needed to go. We stood and shook hands and gave hugs goodbye.

Implications

Speaking about Allah's permission for Isa's miracles has led to pushback from some believers living in Muslim countries. To them, it feels as though we are undermining the divinity of Jesus to agree with the Qur'an and say that he did them "with Allah's permission." But that is exactly what Jesus himself taught:

Therefore Jesus answered and was saying to them, "Truly, truly, I say to you, the Son can do nothing of Himself, unless it is something He sees the Father doing; for whatever the Father does, these things the Son also does in like manner.

—*John 5:19, NASB*

And again in verse 30:

"I can do nothing on My own initiative. As I hear, I judge; and My judgment is just, because I do not seek My own will, but the will of Him who sent Me.

—*John 5:30, NASB*

Jesus had completely submitted himself to the will of the Father as the Philippians 2:7 *kenosis* passage illustrates. Being completely divine and completely human, he emptied himself of his independent use of his divine attributes. In this sense, he totally submitted himself to the will of the Father, even to the point of death.

In the setting of this story, it was key to honor my host who had gotten me access to this family. I wanted to give as much light as he was willing to distribute but only what he was comfortable to reflect. In Luke 10:1–12, Jesus instructed his disciples to stay in the households of those who "returned peace" to them. This peace is more than those who said "hello" in return to a greeting. This peace is those who responded positively to the offer of "shalom" in their lives. If they did not respond to the disciples' offer of peace, the disciples were supposed to shake the dust off their feet and move on.

I offered peace through my story about Jesus. It was possible that peace would not be returned to me after I discussed the sinless nature of Jesus. I was careful to continue only after they received what I had to offer.

Chapter 9

Shop Owner Story Time

Arriving in a new Muslim country is always fun: similar cultural behaviors with new twists. Sometimes the clothes are different. Sometimes the washing ritual is different. The language or dialect is always different—and the people are very different. Each people group has their unique gifts, qualities, and shortcomings.

In the country of this particular trip, they had opted for hyper-Pharisaism. When Jesus had called the religious leaders "white-washed tombs," he likely was referencing their outer clothing that shone in great contrast to their heart. This country was not just white-washed; they were starched.

Everyone kept their thobes in pristine condition all day long. I marveled at how sitting on them didn't seem to leave wrinkles. Their checkered headdresses were a bit more complicated to keep perfect. I saw many of the men repeatedly adjusting the scarf. They also didn't seem to turn their heads very much.

I had been there several days and had engaged in many good training opportunities in private settings with the believers who live and work there and who regularly rub shoulders with these "starched" Muslims. My host, having seen value in my approach of using the Qur'an, said he would like to see how it worked in a public setting. I suggested the market, or *souk*, and he readily agreed.

Sharing about Isa was usually considered off-limits in this country. It enforced very strict rules with well known consequences, especially for ex-pats, if they were caught leading a local astray from his ancestor's faith. Public sharing of faith was almost not possible. Or so my hosts thought.

It was after dark, and we drove to the center of the city where it was obvious that the night life had begun. Not the night life you would see in a Western city. No, this was quite different. The first part of the market had men lining the streets and selling every kind of pet you can imagine: parrots, macaws, falcons, rabbits, snakes, pigeons, dogs, cats, fish, and many creatures I couldn't identify.

Around the next corner was a long street of outdoor cafés with juices, coffees, teas, and local cuisine. Hawkers on the next street obviously catered to the tourist and sold ornate boxes, knives, mosaics, carpets, and local traditional clothes. And the following corner put on a colorful and fragrant display, bag after bag, of bulk spices. Every turn was an experience of sensory overload.

My host had something he wanted to buy, which is always the best way to get into a conversation in the market (whether you actually need the item or not). We found the street that had what he was looking for, and after ducking in and out of several shops, we landed in one that had the styles and colors that would suffice.

It seemed we spent twenty minutes browsing in the store, though I doubt it was that long. But we did look at nearly every item in the place. We asked the owner lots of questions, such as (1) Where was it made? (2) How much is the price? (3) Is that the lowest price? (4) Does this come in any other sizes? (5) What does this do? and (6) How long have you had this shop?

Once you ask these question for several dozen items in earnest as you try to find exactly the right thing, a rapport develops. It spawns other small conversations along the way. It also shows the storekeeper your budget and level of affluence.

It was at this point in our shopping adventure that my host did as perfect of a job as possible to set up the spiritual conversation.

He turned to me and said, "You have a lot of stories. I bet Parwez would love to hear one."

"Stories?" I queried, trying not to sound too eager. "Which story do you think is best?"

"I don't know. Maybe one from the Qur'an?" he replied.

"Oh, yes," I said. "He might like the Path to paradise story." I turned my attention to the shopkeeper. "You know surah Al-Imran, don't you? The Path to paradise begins in aya 55 of Holy Qur'an. The prophet Mohammed (PBUH) wrote that it was Allah who offered Isa as a qurban. That is why it says, 'Allah mutawafeeka Isa.'"

"There were three qurban that Allah provided. One for Adam (PBUH) after he ate the forbidden fruit, the one in place of Ibrahim's son (PBUH), and the last and greatest one, when he sacrificed his blameless Holy Lamb, Isa al Masih (PBUH)."

At this moment in the conversation, Parwez seemed to sense where this was going. He was listening intently and did not want the conversation to end, but he did want to make sure he knew who else was listening.

When we began the story, his back was to the entrance of the small shop. I was about midway in, facing the door. At the mention of a sacrifice, he began slowly taking steps, one at a time, toward the back of the store. I slowly obliged his nonverbal request, and before moving on to the next part of my story, I had repositioned myself with my back to the door.

I continued, "We know Masih Isa (PBUH) was blameless and holy because he didn't have an earthly father. All of the children of Adam (PBUH) have the problem that he started. They began killing one another from the beginning and continue to do that to this day. All those in the line of Adam give the problem to the next generation. If we receive the qurban of Masih Isa, we can have our sin and shame removed and be guaranteed a place in paradise. That's my paradise story!"

He stood quietly at the completion of my story, neither seeming to accept or reject. After a few moments of awkward silence, I turned the conversation back to the coffee mugs that I was interested in purchasing. My host, who had slipped out during the conversation, had reappeared by this time and had more questions about the ornate box he wanted to purchase. He eventually decided against it. I, though, bought one mug, and we left.

"That was brilliant!" I exclaimed as we walked down the street, now out of earshot of Parwez. "You could not have set that up any better. You know, if I lived here, we could really be a great team. I just wish we could have a second conversation with that guy. I think he heard the message."

We walked further, and soon my host's phone rang. It was the friend in the United States for whom he had been shopping. After discussing the size, quality, and price, his friend thousands of miles away decided he would purchase the box. I was elated. We had a reason to go back.

Retracing our steps, we were soon standing in Parwez's shop, negotiating over the box that my host had last examined. When my host's phone rang again, there was another slight pause in the conversation, which gave Parwez a moment to ask me follow-up questions, questions that I had heard many times before.

"Are you a Christian or a Muslim?" came the typical inquiry.

"Actually, I'm submitted to Allah through the qurban of Isa al Masih (PBUH). Followers of Isa try to obey his teachings rather than the teachings of denominations." He gave no response to my description of a follower. Sadly, we departed the shop with plans to return to him on the next trip.

Implications

Asking a Muslim if they are familiar with a surah of the Qur'an does several things. First, it lets you know where that the person is coming from religiously. Most often, you will have someone glancing to the floor or looking away because they do not know what their book says. This gives you an opportunity, due to a slight pause in your audience's thinking, to present them something they are supposed to know. Even if your audience is aware of what it says, they will have never heard it the way you are presenting it.

Secondly, it tells them that you are familiar with their holy book and you are not offended by it. Most Muslims believe that followers of Jesus are antagonistically opposed to the Qur'an. Their inability to hear the gospel comes from a cultural block about books and tradition, rather than truth. When you show you are not afraid to quote from the Qur'an, it opens their ears, minds, and hearts.

The Christian presence in most Muslim countries is dominated by heavy traditions of Christians bowing before icons, statues, and pictures. Muslims believe that placing images of prophets and saints on dashboards and around places of worship, even in homes, is a common practice for a Christian. Much like Orthodox Judaism, which strictly adheres to the Law of Moses, Muslims think it is idolatry to have any type of graven image. They consider it blasphemy to have a representation of any of the prophets, including Jesus and Muhammad.

Separating ourselves from the existing Christian culture, no matter how accurate or inaccurate it may be, is very important so that the Muslim audience is able to hear the message. Jesus himself is the focus, not a particular manifestation of the way people choose to follow him. His perfect, holy sacrifice on our behalf is the gospel. What followers look like and how they choose to identify themselves after coming to faith is a discipleship issue that comes after that decision.

Talking about ISA

Chapter 10
Imam's Unlikely Chant

Muslims have a presence in every major city on earth. In some areas, their numbers are growing exponentially. With your trusty smartphone in hand, it is now possible to locate a mosque anywhere you travel. They are usually not far away, and you may be very surprised at what you will find inside.

While attending a conference at a highly traveled city far south of the equator, it seemed a must to visit a local mosque. Providentially, the oldest mosque in the city was within walking distance of my hotel.

A friend and I entered the mosque and took our position opposite a group of men who were gathered to socialize. As prayers began, we faced the appropriate direction, which was diagonal in relationship to the street, and began going through the Muslim prayer postures.

My traveling companion's first response after finishing was how humbling it felt to talk to God on your knees and with your forehead touching the carpet. It is truly a much different experience than merely closing your eyes.

After prayers we slowly drifted over to the group of local men and sat quietly, noting features of the mosque and smiling when bits of English made the conversation understandable. Their dialogue finally started to trail off, and it seemed that they had inserted space to see if the visitors had something to say. When several glances said, "We welcome you for input," I began to introduce the topic I had hoped to cover.

"Your museum attached next door and the history of your people is fascinating. The centuries that you have faithfully continued in this location is truly a testament to the faithfulness of Allah. I've had the privilege of praying in mosques in several countries. Few have recorded their heritage as well as you have."

"We are followers of Masih Isa (PBUH) because of what the prophet Muhammad (PBUH) wrote in Al-Imran 3:55: 'Allah mutawafeeka Isa.' Allah offered Isa as qurban for the removal of sin and shame. The reason Allah was able to do this was because Isa (PBUH) was blameless and holy. We know he was blameless and holy since he was born to the virgin Maryam."

At this point, actually even before I finished the last few words, the imam sitting to our right, broke out into an Arabic chant. Assuming he was chanting something I had stirred in him, I sat quietly waiting for him to finish so I could continue. He never did. I learned later that he was the oldest imam in the city and very well respected. I leaned to the young man to my left and asked what the imam was quoting. His reply was quite surprising.

"Imam is quoting the Gospel of John in Arabic," he said.

"Really?" I said softly and slowly. "Why is he doing this?"

"The piece of property our mosque was built on several centuries ago was donated by a Christian businesswoman. Because of that act of kindness, we have always honored those in the Christian faith."

"Very nice," I whispered, trying to hide my outright surprise at the result of a three-hundred-year-old act of kindness.

The imam continue for several more minutes and then trailed off. Another young man got up slowly and made his way to a microphone situated in the corner of the room in the direction the men faced during prayers. He spoke into it and began the call the prayer (see appendix C).

Not feeling led this time to participate in salaat, I stood and began shaking hands with as many as possible. I removed a business card that I had collected from the reception desk of the hotel where we were staying and handed it to the man who had sat to my left. We made our way toward the door, where I stopped and stared in amazement at the poster that was mounted to the right. What first caught my eye was the white lamb.

Even more amazing was the word qurbani printed in larger type than the rest. The poster requested donations for poor Muslim families so they could purchase a lamb or goat for the upcoming *Eid*.

I took out my phone, snapped a photo of the poster and continued out the door toward my hotel, praying that someone would show up at the hotel later with questions needing answers. No one did.

Implications

Interjecting yourselves socially into any subculture is an art form that takes grace and tact. No one likes to be bulldozed by outsiders, especially when it's in an environment of practicing your faith.

Usually all that is necessary to open a door is a willingness to be observant and humble. In this case, a museum attached to the mosque gave us a legitimate reason to enter. Although you will not always have this obvious a reason to enter, a normal, natural reason usually will become evident with a little bit of observation and inquisitiveness. Asking a question about something new you learned about Islam or to obtain clarity about a verse you have read in the Qur'an are natural incursions. Whatever your means of interjecting, the more humble and less abrasive it is, the better.

Islam is more diverse than Christianity. That concept is easy to overlook when it appears Muslims all pray in the same fashion in buildings that are relatively similar in design. The above story shows just how different they can be in their traditions.

Please do not misunderstand me to say that these Muslims who knew the Gospel of John were believers. I do not think that they were. Once you understand that Islam is more about cultural forms (dress, language, prayer postures, reciting of text), and less about theology, you will start to gain a different understanding of who they are.

Many Westerners mistakenly think that the Qur'an provides the detail for the behaviors being displayed by Muslims around the world. It is just not that simple. Local customs as well as teachings from previous imams and other books within Islam create uniqueness country-to-country. When you encounter people who identify themselves as Muslim, you never know what you are going to get.

Chapter 11
Member of Parliament and the Trinity

Often God puts us next to someone who holds a unique station in life. Having boarded a small commuter plane, I conversed with the gentleman packed tightly next to me on the plane. Before arriving at my desired destination, the flight would make one stop: this man's city.

After learning he was an MP (Member of Parliament), something similar to a US Congressman, I inquired how things were in his province. I knew that his constituency was split fifty/fifty between Muslim and Christian. So I thought I would gently delve into the ongoing struggle that occasionally made the news.

He explained, "Things are always in constant friction. There are struggles over property, struggles over business territory, and struggles between families. It can be quite difficult."

"I'm very sorry to hear that," I said. "You have been entrusted with a very difficult task. May I apologize on behalf of all Christians?"

His face was bewildered at such an offer. I can only presume that the followers of Jesus he knew were usually putting blame on the Muslims in his area while not accepting responsibility for their own actions. As for me, I had a much different reason to make that statement than the current political problem.

"What do you mean?" he asked with great curiosity.

"Well, when I read the Holy Qur'an," I explained, pausing slightly for effect, "I have noticed that Allah is mentioned repeatedly."

"Yes, of course. That is God," he said.

"But I also noticed there is someone else called '*Kalimatullah*,' or the 'Word of God.'"

"Oh yes, that is Jesus," he said.

"But then it talks about another concept that enabled Adam (PBUH) to come alive in the garden—the Ruah Allah, or Spirit of God," I said.

"Yes, we know the Ruah Allah, the life-giving Spirit of God," he said.

"So there is Allah, Kalimatullah, and the Ruah Allah," I summarized. "How is it that these three work together?"

"Masha'allah," he exclaimed. "We don't know. It's a miracle!"

"Exactly. Please forgive us for thinking we can explain a miracle," I said humbly.

"I've never met a Christian like you." he replied.

Implications

I know that I did not present the gospel to this man. The way of introducing the tri-unity of our God might even bother you a little bit. My intention was not only to put Jesus in the same realm as God and the Spirit but also to show that man that not all followers of Jesus are more interested in converting than they are in showing love.

Sometimes the most gentle and innocent way of elevating Jesus to your Muslim friend will send them on a journey to explore what they have not previously thought to do. Anytime you provide the full explanation of Jesus's person, his work, and his offer of salvation, it is obviously best. But not all conversations grant that opportunity, and God's Spirit does not always give us freedom to do so.

This man heard from his own holy book that there are three different aspect of Allah's deity: God, his Word, and his Spirit. Perhaps opening his eyes to this revelation will not only make him less antagonistic to Christian constituents who insist on pressing him with Trinitarian thinking, but also will give him pause in his own understanding of the miraculous nature of God.

Chapter 12
Dinner with a Friend's Friend

As I drove to a US city where I would be conducting a training event the next day, I contacted an educational consultant whom I originally had met several months before and that lived in a nearby town. She excitedly arranged for me to meet her Turkish friend within an hour of my arrival into the city. Delighted, I pushed the speed limit the entire ten-hour trip to get there as early as possible.

Yusef was eager to continue the spiritual dialogue that the consultant had started with him at the local mall. He worked there at a kiosk, and she would stop by once a week to greet him and his workmates, all of whom were Turkish Muslims. Since she traveled regularly to the Middle East, she regularly enjoyed the hospitality of nationals there, and she wanted to return that gift to those visiting her country.

So she had invited a group of Muslims over to her house for dinner early that month.

When I arrived in the city, I found the restaurant she had indicated and met both of them waiting inside. Once we had gotten our plates of food at the buffet, I tried to limit my conversation. This consultant had built rapport with Yusef, and I wanted him to feel as comfortable as possible with the new person at the table. In addition, I needed to wait for a natural bridge to a spiritual conversation to occur. We finished our first plate, and I excused myself for a few seconds to spoon a second helping at the buffet. Then I returned to join the small talk. My friend did a nice job of getting caught up on the current events of Yusef's life and his friends.

She introduced me as someone who also travels prolifically to other countries and whose hobbies were studying and teaching the four holy books: the *Torat*, the *Zabur*, the *Injil*, and the Holy Qur'an. This seemed a natural segue for why I was about to articulate a certain story.

I began, "I'm a follower of Isa al Masih because of what Muhammad the prophet (PBUH) recorded in the third surah of the Holy Qur'an. It has to do with Isa (PBUH) not having an earthly father. There was only one other person, the prophet Adam (PBUH), who didn't have an earthly father. He walked with Allah in paradise until he ate the forbidden fruit, setting off a problem in his lineage. This problem was immediately noticeable when Cain killed Abel. But what is more important to realize is that the children of Adam (PBUH) passed the problem to their children and even their grandchildren. It is evident that all in the line of Adam (PBUH) even up till now still retain the problem started from eating the forbidden fruit. We know this because the children of Adam (PBUH) are still killing one another. The key to Isa (PBUH) not having an earthly father is that he was not a recipient of Adam's problem. He is completely sinless and holy."

Yusef agreed, "It is true that Isa did not have an earthly father."

"Peace be upon him," I interjected, keeping the appropriate title in place.

"But in fact," Yusef countered, "Adam (PBUH) had neither father nor mother, so he is very much like Isa."

I responded, "Oh yes, he did have creaturely perfection, I completely agree. After all, he walked with Allah in paradise."

Yusef continued, "Since Adam (PBUH) was created from clay, and did not have a mother, he was very pure. He could be considered to be more pure than Isa, since he had neither father nor mother."

"However," I countered, "the major difference between Adam (PBUH) and Isa (PBUH) is that it was clearly shown that Adam was able to sin because he ate the forbidden fruit. This caused him to be removed from the presence of Allah. For only one sin, he was removed from paradise. It says in Holy Qur'an surah 7 that Adam tried to make leaves to cover his nakedness, but it didn't work, and Allah had to clothe him. Isa (PBUH) never sinned. He was tempted the same as Adam (PBUH) but remained sinless. This would be very important for Allah to be able to offer him as qurban. Qurban is the way Allah has always dealt with sin and shame."

"We know Isa never died," Yusef said. "It was not him on the cross; it was someone who looked very similar. Isa was actually taken to heaven alive."

"I didn't know that," I said, puzzled. "I thought the prophet Muhammad (PBUH) recorded the reason for the death of Isa in Al Imran, aya 55. It says, 'Allah mutawafeeka Isa,' or, 'God caused Jesus to die.' If Isa never died, then aren't we still trapped by our sin and still unable to be in Allah's presence?"

Yusef answered matter of factly, "Actually, Allah can just forgive sin by saying, 'forgiven.' He does not have to kill someone to forgive our sin."

Looking perplexed once again, I said, "I agree Allah can forgive sin, but I guess I don't understand on what basis can he forgive? He is not like a corrupt judge in a court who can be bribed not to punish wrong behavior. Allah is completely just. He is completely holy. To say he can forgive sin without applying the penalty would be contrary to his nature."

"Allah is merciful. Allah can forgive because he can do anything. He can merely say it, and it is done," Yusef explained.

"So Allah does not have to punish sin?" I queried. "This seems to make him into a corrupted judge. I agree that he is Merciful. Masha'allah. *Bismillah al-rahman al-rahim*. But Allah is also completely holy. And to say that he can turn aside and not punish sin would make him corrupt. He is merciful, but he is completely just as well. His justice and mercy create a complication. The answer to the dilemma is to show his people mercy and to pour out his wrath on the blameless Holy Lamb, Masih Isa. Isa was offered as qurban."

Yusef seemed put off at this. He was somewhat perplexed about how to answer. He repeated again that Isa never died and that Allah could forgive sin by just saying "forgiven." I did not contradict him this time. I let him talk as long as he wanted, and even when there was a pause, I retained eye contact and waited for him to continue. He was floundering and looking for a way out, and I was going to be patient and allow him to find a way to save face. He eventually found his out for the topic. "Have you ever heard of Zakir Naik?" he asked.

"No, I haven't heard of him. Is he an imam?" I responded.

"Yes, a very, very sharp man. He has converted thousands from Christianity." Yusef said with excitement.

"Wow. I've never heard. Is he here in the United States?" I asked.

"He is actually in India. He is a very brilliant man. He can answer all of your questions. He converts Christians to Islam all the time," said Yusef.

"I will Google him and find him on YouTube," I replied. "I will make sure to find him. Thank you for letting me know about him."

By now we had finished our dinner, and the conversation turned back to my friend and Yusef. My friend made him feel comfortable and accepted, recalling memories of his time at her house along with his other friends. She concluded by inviting them again when they had a free evening for another home-cooked American meal.

We made our way outside to the sidewalk and shook hands warmly. I thanked him repeatedly for all that he had shared and said that I would be thinking about our conversation for some time. We traded text messages to ensure we had each other's phone number, and I told him that if I ever got back to his city, I would love to have dinner again.

Implications

In almost all of the stories you have read thus far, there was a great hesitancy to continue without permission. You also might have sensed that there was almost a hesitation to give more truth unless there was a receptive response. Every situation is slightly different, but the person-of-peace principle from Luke 10:1–12 still holds true.

The principle in Luke 10 is that the person who responds positively to a spiritual concept gets more spiritual truth. Those who reject truth get less. Arguments usually ensue when we try to overcome multiple objections from individuals who are not interested.

This conversation might have felt different in that there were several back and forth exchanges that seemed to be a debate. What is missing from the written picture is his tone and his nonverbal communication. There was an earnestness about his comments and questions that showed he was trying to save face but at the same time gaining new understanding.

There was never a moment in the dialogue when his emotions began to get involved. He never raised his voice. In turn, I was also very calm, nodded, gave positive affirmation verbally when I could. But I expressed puzzlement when I didn't understand how his position could work practically based on the character of God.

It is helpful to understand that the concepts I shared with him were completely new to him. He had never heard these things before. If I were to tell you the Statue of Liberty was a replica of an ancient Egyptian goddess called Maat, who keeps things in balance, you might be perplexed. What you knew from your childhood would be contradicted with a new idea.

Once you receive a new concept, you have a choice. Defend your own view by dismissing the new view as crazy, immediately adopt the view, or begin research into the evidence that brought questions to your own view.

Most Muslims will defend against a new perspective about Jesus, his sacrifice, and the path to paradise. This does not mean in all cases that they are rejecting your message. They might be hiding embarrassment or, in other words, removing the shame they feel.

The task, or art form, is to discern through nonverbal and verbal cues whether to keep going or not. This is where our spiritual walk and the ability to hear from God's Spirit come into play. Many things block our ability to hear God's voice: lack of prayer before entering a spiritual battle, unconfessed sin, pride and arrogance, to name a few.

Not every turndown of your admiration of Jesus is a sign to stop. Many times it is, but not always. Sometimes the person is absorbing the truth but culturally isn't able to let you know. Walking with the Spirit while sharing in his power and remaining calm in the face of honest objections are all important to successful sharing.

Chapter 13

The Whole Truth with No More Rebuttal

Walking into a small wholesale grocery store in the Persian Gulf, it immediately became apparent the store wasn't for everyday shoppers. Three desks were arranged around the walls and bulk products lined the shelves behind them: candy, coffee, cookies, and packages with Arabic scribbles that I couldn't make out. "Asalaam wa aleikum," I rambled quickly, trying to sound local and friendly.

"*Aleikum salaam wa rahmatullahi wa barakatuh*," came the reply. Not only did I get peace back, but mercy and the blessings of Allah.

"Do you have dates?" I asked, reaching into my carry-on to find a sample package. I had been trudging around with three shopping bags in 105 degree heat in the middle of the day while visiting a Gulf city.

He replied, "No, we don't have." Then, seeing the small box I was holding up, he added, "Yes, I know what you mean."

"OK," I said, "*Shokran lek*," and turned to go out the door.

As I began to make a 180-degree turn, he asked, "Are you a Muslim?"

Ramadan and dates are quite the combination. I had underestimated the value of having dates on my person when entering the country. For instance, I received a smile from the security agent when she she saw them through the X-ray. When I asked the customs agents where to buy them, he merely replied, "They are always at my house. Come by my house later and have some." Now, by asking for dates in a grocery store, it brought up a question about what faith I followed.

"I'm a follower of Isa al Masih, (PBUH)," I replied.

"Ah, you're a Christian," came the predictable reply.

"No, not really. Those people sometimes pray to idols and worship images. I don't believe in that. I'm a follower of Isa as revealed in the third surah of Holy Qur'an, Al-Imran."

"I've never heard of that," he said. I took the opportunity to approach his desk and have a seat while he continued, "The difference between you and me is that I pray directly to Allah. How do you pray?"

I replied, "I pray to Allah in the name of Isa al Masih (PBUH)."

"So you need a bridge. I don't need a bridge to pray directly to Allah," he said.

So I said, "Well, for certain we need a qurban. I can't get to Allah without a qurban. This is what it says in Holy Qur'an. You know it says in the third surah that Isa al Masih (PBUH) was born to a virgin name Maryam. He was the only one after the prophet Adam (PBUH) without a father. It was a miracle when Isa was placed into the womb of Maryam."

"Yes, we agree. He was placed by the Spirit of Allah," he replied.

"The Ruah Allah," I interjected.

"Yes, he was placed by the Ruah Allah in Maryam, but he was not Allah," he added matter of factly.

"Actually he was Kalimatullah, the Word of God. You know, there is Allah, Kalimatullah, and the Ruah Allah. It is a miracle how they all three work together, but there is only one God." I said.

His face said that he didn't know what to do with that, so I kept going. "So Adam (PBUH) was removed from paradise for only one sin. Adam could not offer *zakat*, or salaat to overcome his sin. He needed a covering. The Holy Qur'an says Allah made clothes for him as the covering for sin and shame. Adam tried to cover his shame by making clothes from leaves (Q 20:121–122). But instead, Allah performed qurban on an animal in order to use the skin for their clothes. This was the first qurban. It shows something has to die to cover sin."

He began smiling at me and then laughed out loud. I looked to the closest man at another desk and said, "He thinks I'm a funny guy."

I returned my attention to the storekeeper, to see his response to my diversion. "No," came my new friend's reply. "I'm not laughing at you. What you are saying is very, very interesting."

He continued to listen, so I kept talking. "The second qurban was provided for Ibrahim when he took his son up the mountain to pass the test of faith. Allah withheld Ibrahim's hand from killing his son and instead provided a ram caught in the bushes. This shows that Allah can provide a substitute qurban, something to die in place of something else."

"But you don't believe Muhammad (PBUH) was a prophet," came his questioning reply, still looking for a way to dismiss my theology.

"Of course I do." His face quickly contorted in astonishment, and he had no reply. "The prophets before Masih Isa (PBUH) all pointed forward to Isa's coming while Muhammad (PBUH) pointed back. That is why Muhammad (PBUH) wrote about Isa, 'Blessed is the day He was born, the day He died, and the day He will be raised back to life' (Q 19:15). The whole point of Masih Isa not having an earthly father was to ensure the qurban would be sinless and holy. You know that after Adam (PBUH) sinned, his children began killing one another. In fact, all the children in the line of Adam (PBUH) even up to this day still have his problem. Masih Isa is the only one in the line who was fatherless. So he can be the only one in the line who was able to be a spotless qurban."

To break any possible tension, I pointed to the shelf behind him and said, "Hey, is that Lavazza coffee? That's my wife's favorite." As he reached to grab a package, I clarified, "The one in the blue packet called Crema. That's it."

"Yes, it's eighty *dirham* for eight packets," he responded. I contorted my face to calculate the exchange rate and do the math, and he went right back to the previous line of questions. "Where did you say you were from?"

I felt as though he was still trying to figure out a way to dismiss the truth after I had neatly avoided all the typical pitfalls. "Houston, Texas," I replied.

"Oh, Houston. And you are doing business here?"

"Just passing through, actually. I'm on my way home now but wanted to take some dates for my friends. They are much better quality and much better prices, especially the Saudi and the Emirati kinds." I thanked him again and began to stand and gather my things. By showing him I was about to leave and to relieve any remaining tension, I concluded the story from earlier.

"To finish the discussion of qurban, there is the third and the greatest qurban that Allah ever performed. It is what was recorded in Al-Imran 3:55: 'Allah mutawafeeka Isa.' This was when Allah offered his blameless Holy Lamb, Isa al Masih. He then raised Isa from the dead, and Isa (PBUH) traveled the straight path all the way to paradise, where he is now waiting to come back. If you receive the qurban of Isa al Masih for the removal of your sin and shame, you can be assured a place in paradise."

"Thank you for the very interesting lesson. I really enjoyed it," he said sincerely.

"You are very welcome. Where did you say I could find these dates? At a supermarket near here?"

Implications

This dialogue may have caused you to be more uncomfortable. You probably thought, "Did he really just answer a Muslim with agreement that Muhammad (PBUH) was a prophet?"

I can think of few characters in modern history that bring more emotion to the mind of Western evangelicals than the Prophet Muhammad. We have all heard how he married a nine year old, promoted warring raids on his opponents, not to mention started a world-wide faith that squashes Christianity and commits horrendous crimes in the name of God. That's more than enough to cause consternation.

In my attempt to explain why I said, "Yes, I believe Muhammad (PBUH) was a prophet," please do not read that I'm excusing any of these purported actions. If they happened, they are sin—sin at the same level as Moses killing an Egyptian and David taking Bathsheba and then cleverly disposing of her husband, Uriah the Hittite.

As you noticed in my response to this Muslim, I supported my understanding of Muhammad being called a prophet based upon the idea that in his book, he alluded to the death of Jesus and the resurrection, not to mention that he also included 104 verses about Jesus, twenty-five of which referred to him as "Jesus the Messiah." In the Qur'an, Jesus is called

- the Word of God;
- the one closest to God;
- the Spirit of God;
- the Truth; and
- the Way.

In addition, the Qur'an records in the nineteenth surah, in aya 33 that Jesus said, *"Peace be upon me the day I was born, the day I die, and the day I shall be raised to life."*

Of course Islam does not teach, believe, or quote these kinds of truths. Many passages in the Qur'an, including those that teach violence only in self-defense are conveniently avoided. But what does this have to do with Muhammad and whether or not he is a prophet?

Historically, except for traditions that were recorded generations after his death, there is very little from the actual lifetime of Muhammad. Granted, traditions are often true and are carried forth because of stories from people who witness these events, but it does not mean they are all true.

At the end of the day, the real question we have to wrestle in regard to presenting the gospel to our Muslim friends would be this: Am I willing to argue over a belief from another culture that can never be empirically proven either way when it has no bearing on a person's eternal salvation?

A person can believe that any one of the modern faith healers, celebrity preachers, or a scientist is a prophet from God. Their belief in this person as a prophet has no bearing on their eternal salvation. One's salvation is based solely on whether or not they have accepted Jesus's finished work on the cross on their behalf. Of course if the prophet you are following is leading you away from this truth, then that prophet can be very harmful. But if it can be shown that they point to Jesus as the way to paradise, that prophet's words would be a significant means for bringing understanding to the gospel message.

If the person you are following directs you to faith in Christ, then whether or not they are a prophet is irrelevant. And if the people group you happen to be working with has an extremely high regard for the writings that have been attributed to this person, you should want to use that as an open door to the gospel. When a Muslim is gently confronted with the fact that Muhammad (PBUH) recorded God's sacrifice of Jesus, it is very strong piece of evidence they must consider.

Chapter 14

Eggs Lead to Eternal Life

Browsing through a weekend market soon led me to a display of bleached-white ostrich eggs with Arabic script wrapped around them like black bands. The only logical reason for Arabic script in the particular country I was in would be verses from Qur'an. My questions would soon prove the assumption correct.

"Asalaam wa aleikum," I said as I stopped to examine the eggs.

"Aleikum salaam," came the predictable reply.

"These must be verses from Holy Qur'an," I said with delight. "I am a follower of Isa al Masih. May I tell you about my favorite passage in the Qur'an?"

"Yes," the man said, with readiness in his voice.

"Isa Al Masih was born to a virgin named Maryam according to surah 3, aya 42. This was very important.

Were there any other prophets that did not have an earthly father?"

"Yes, the prophet Adam, did not have an earthly father," he responded thoughtfully.

"Exactly. Adam was created when Allah took clay from the ground and formed it into the shape of man, breathed on it, and it became alive," I said.

With every new thought and every new sentence, my willing audience only nodded. His eyes got brighter and wider. There was never a wrinkled brow nor a questioning look.

Unhindered, I began again, "Adam walked in paradise with Allah until something went very wrong. His children began killing one another. Even worse, the problem with his children was passed on to their children. In fact, everyone in the line of Adam received the problem that he started. Even now, the descendants of Adam are still killing one another all around the world."

Again more nods and a sense of expectancy of more good things to come. Any hesitation I had about talking to a Muslim selling verses of the Qur'an was completely gone, and I felt myself getting more and more excited as the story continued.

"But there is one in the line of Adam who did not inherit the problem that Adam started. Only one in the line of Adam was sinless and holy. Isa al Masih was born of a virgin and was without blemish.

"It then says that Masih Isa was able to heal men who were born blind, the only prophet who was able to do so. It continues in the third surah that Masih Isa could also raise dead at Allah's direction, the only prophet in Holy Qur'an who could do this, and the only prophet that could create life.

"Masih Isa took clay from the ground when he was but a small boy and made a bird from it. He then breathed on the clay, and the bird took flight and left his hands.

"All these things made Masih Isa different than any of the other prophets. The ability to heal the sick, raise the dead, and create life made him very, very special. In fact, since he was blameless, sinless, and holy, he was the only descendant of Adam with those qualities," I said.

Still expecting him to push back, I paused to catch my breath and see what he would say. There was again no reply. Only lips parted, eyes wide open.

So I went on, "When we reach aya 55, you will notice it says, 'Allah mutawafeeka Isa.' That means it was Allah who caused Isa to die. I know you have heard of surah 4:157 where it says, *'they killed him not, nor did they crucify Him, but so it was made to appear to them as so.'* This is actually true. It appeared that the Jews and the Romans killed Isa, but they did not. It was actually Allah who offered him as a qurban.

"You are familiar with the three qurban? The first was offered for Adam after he was kicked out of paradise for only one sin. Just one sin and he could not walk with Allah. Adam tried to fashion clothes for himself out of leaves to cover his sin and shame, but Allah said that he must clothe him. So Allah performed qurban on a spotless lamb and covered the sin and shame with the skin of the animal.

"The second qurban was provided for Ibrahim when he took his son up the mountain. Allah stopped him from sacrificing his son and, instead, showed him a ram caught in the bushes. That is because Allah can provide a substitute qurban. He can provide something to die in place of someone else.

"But the third and the greatest qurban was what the prophet Muhammad (PBUH) wrote about in 3:55. Allah offered his blameless, Holy Lamb Isa al Masih as the final qurban to remove all our sin and all our shame. If you receive the qurban of Masih Isa, you can be guaranteed a place in paradise."

There was never a moment in my presentation that he broke eye contact. He never wrinkled his brow or objected.

After I completed my explanation of the qurban, his reply was certain and clear. "Yes, I do want the qurban of Masih Isa."

I replied, "Then Isa's qurban has removed your sin and shame. Masih Isa says that you are now a part of his kingdom, and you can never be removed."

"Can you get me a Bible?" he asked.

The shock from his statement must have been all over my face. I had not mentioned Christianity, churches, or the Bible in my talk about Jesus. "Certainly," I replied. "But may I ask why you want one?"

"If I am going to follow Isa, I need to know what he says," the man told me.

I asked if he was going to be there at the market the next morning, and I told him I would be back with what would be his new prized possession. We also exchanged e-mail and phone numbers to stay in touch.

Over the next months, I sent him verses of Scripture with questions, to which he readily replied. This pattern went on seamlessly until one day I did not get a reply for one of my e-mails. Thinking something was wrong, I sent a text message to his phone. The answer came back promptly. He had found a group of believers who were meeting in an apartment and was being fed with both fellowship and truth. I now understood, without him having to say, why a response to the e-mail had not been sent—he had found a new family.

Implications

In this story, you most likely notice that the typical PBUH is not mentioned after Isa, Abraham, and Adam. My editor did not forget it or leave it out. In this case, for whatever reason, I did not use the phrase, and it worked fine. Perhaps this was because this particular country was less strict, but I can't give you a solid reason.

Here in the States, I had a friend take me to lunch with his Palestinian friend to hear the explanation of Jesus from the Qur'an. He listened intently and with great respect. I expected him to come to faith in Jesus as well, but he did not. We parted ways, and he walked to the car with his friend. I learned later the one thing that impressed the Palestinian the most was that I had said, "Peace be upon him," for every mention of a prophet. I say that because it is generally a good idea to add PBUH.

Similarly, not in all countries, areas of towns, or even apartment complexes is it safe to hand out a physical copy of the Bible. The visible paper expression of God's word leads to unnecessary persecution. There are many ways to get the Scriptures to a new believer in the twenty-first century without using paper.

This particular country was not a high-risk area, and I quickly obliged in giving him a Bible. You might be wondering that if the country was so open, why even present the gospel from the Qur'an to begin with? The answer lies in third-generation thinking.

Anytime we present the gospel, we should be thinking beyond the person who is standing in front of us to those they will soon share with, and even more so, to the ones that these recipients have access to pass on the gospel. Many of their family members will have relatives back home in a limited-access country. It is best to be wise in sharing an example that could be easily reproducible, even for the second and third person down the line.

These first generation believers should be treated exactly as if they were still back home. This trains them to know how to share with family, perhaps even over the phone, in a way that is reproducible beyond where they currently live.

Conclusion

I must confess there are large pieces of information missing from these pages that can only be learned by personally observing someone engaging with lost people. Jesus's style of discipleship was walking three years with the disciples. It isn't just a cliché to say that how to fish is learned by observing, not just through information transmittal. It is caught more than taught.

Knowing when to continue and when not to push a Muslim is something that must be directed by the Holy Spirit. You probably felt when you read many of the encounters that it didn't go far enough, or that I didn't press the issue hard enough. Body language, tone, and eye contact often determine when a person is open.

In my experience with eleven occasions when a Muslim has come to faith during the first conversation, it was very obvious where things were going. These conversations were with a Muslim in Mali, with a Turk in Iraq, an Egyptian in his hometown, an Afghan in Athens, a Swahili in East Africa, and an up-country Tanzanian.

The idea is to talk boldly about Jesus and see who is drawn like a paper clip to a magnet. Not only do we have very few people actually fishing, but the majority have spent most of their time with the wrong people. We invest our time with those who like us, who are like us, and who enjoy doing the things we like to do.

The model for discipleship, as well as for those who need the gospel, is to search for those who respond to spiritual truth. We often mistake nice people for those who are being drawn to Christ. We all like nice people. We should all have nice friends. However, our focus is to be looking for those who either want to know more, or if they have already come to faith, are putting into practice what they are learning.

You will have undoubtedly noticed the absence of blaspheming or denigrating the prophet Muhammad or the Islamic holy book. Neither did I critique Islam. There is more than enough of that approach out there. I prefer to follow Paul's respectful methodology that he not only clearly displayed in Acts 17 on Mars Hill, but also reiterated in Acts 19:35–37 through the response of the town clerk:

[35] After quieting the crowd, the town clerk said, "Men of Ephesus, what man is there after all who does not know that the city of the Ephesians is guardian of the temple of the great Artemis and of the image which fell down

from heaven? ³⁶ *So, since these are undeniable facts, you ought to keep calm and to do nothing rash.* ³⁷ <u>*For you have brought these men here who are neither robbers of temples nor blasphemers of our goddess.*</u>

—*NASB (emphasis added)*

We can exalt Jesus, without denigrating things which cause offense. That does not mean we don't clearly explain that by our own efforts or works we are incapable of getting to heaven. We should—and we should with clarity and hopefully with much conviction and passion. However, to blaspheme a person or a system unnecessarily clouds our message of a preeminent Christ.

When they see him for who he is, and what he has done, you don't have to wrestle the old system from them. The beauty of the burden that Islam puts on people is once they are free of it, they are no longer interested in its merits. This brings us to our next step in the process: What do we do after they say, "yes?"

There is as much disagreement on this topic as there is on how to share Jesus. As a Westerner in a foreign culture, I am painfully aware that I will never understand the deep world view issues of being raised in a Muslim culture. I can only imagine the result of a Saudi raised Muslim who comes to faith, moves to the United States, and then begins telling a Western-raised evangelical all that is wrong with their practice of faith. I doubt that would go very well.

Neither do we want to lead them to faith and leave them on their own. We should note that there is a philosophical difference between becoming the "theological answer man" for a new believer, and helping him to learn to ask God and to be sensitive to the Holy Spirit's voice.

To give a practical example, in one Middle Eastern city several house churches whose members have the same Muslim background have developed two different cultural viewpoints on dress. One has adopted entirely Western clothing because of their location in the city, the relationships from which they came, and their own preference. The women are not covered in their house meetings nor do they cover their heads in public.

The other group looks very much like a traditional Muslim gathering. The woman all cover. The neighborhood where they reside makes it impossible culturally for them to look Western.

The point is that God calls different people in different settings and from different backgrounds to express their faith in Jesus differently. He is still the spotless Lamb of

God that takes away the sin of the world, but his worship is expressed in ways that are as unique as the people it represents. Even more, their lives are changed by his finished work on the cross to the glory of his name.

Talking about ISA

Appendix A

Asalaam wa aleikum. *Peace be upon you*, the worldwide accepted greeting for Muslims.

ablution. The Muslim ceremonial washing before prayers, which in many countries includes hands, feet, head, face, ears, inside of nose, and a quick gargle in the mouth.

Aleikum salaam (wa rahmatullahi wa barakatuh). *Peace be upon you as well*, the appropriate reply to the worldwide greeting. Sometimes Muslims add *(and the mercy and blessings of God.)*

Alhumdulilah. Arabic for *Thanks be to God.*

Allah. Arabic word for the Creator used by both Arabic-speaking Christians and Muslims. It predates Islam and comes from the Aramaic word *Alaha.*

Al-Imran. The third chapter in the Qur'an, pronounced "Al Eam-ron."

aywa. Arabic for *yes*.

aya. A verse in the Qur'an.

Bismillah al-rahman al-rahim. Arabic for *In the name of God, the most gracious and most merciful.*

corban. In some places, *corbani*; see *qurban* below; originally from the Aramaic, meaning *dedicated to God.*

dhow. An East African *sailboat.*

dirham. a unit of currency in Arab countries.

Eid al Adha. Arabic for *The Festival of the Sacrifice*, an annual event whose date moves every year according to the lunar calendar and which celebrates Abraham's willingness to sacrifice his son.

five pillars. The five acts that bestow righteousness on the doer in Islam: *salute* (prayer), *sawm* (fasting), *hajj* (*pilgrimage*), *zakat* (giving), and *shahade* (belief) articulated as "Allah is One and Muhammad is his prophet."

habibi. *Close male friend.*

hajj. An Islamic pilgrimage to Mecca. Each Muslim is to go on hajj once during his lifetime.

Hawwa. Arabic for Adam's wife *Eve.*

Ibrahim (PBUH). Arabic for *Abraham.*

Injil. The name given in the Qur'an for the written Gospels (Matthew, Mark, Luke, and John).

imam. A spiritual leader who leads prayers in a mosque

Isa Al Masih (PBUH). *Jesus the Messiah* in Arabic, the title used for him twenty-five times in the Qur'an.

Kalimatullah. The *Word of God*, a title given to Jesus in the Qur'an.

madrasa. An elementary school where the Qur'an is taught.

Masha'allah. Arabic for *God did something miraculous.*

minaret. Arabic for *beacon*; also related to *lighthouse*. A tall spire that adorns a mosque where the call to prayer is announced.

Muhammad (PBUH). The traditional founder of the Islamic faith. It is highly disrespectful and unnecessary to engage in any negative dialogue about him as a person.

mutawafeeka. Arabic, lit. *to cause someone else's death*, pronounced "moo tah wa fee' kah." Comes from the root verb *wafat*, meaning "to die."

Nsha'allah. Arabic for *If God is willing*; sometimes used as an excuse for not following through with a request.

paradise. In the mind of a Muslim, paradise is synonymous with the Garden of Eden. Paradise is the hope of every obedient Muslim.

PBUH. *Peace be upon him*, the respectful way to mention a prophet from the Bible or Qur'an in Islam. Every time a prophet's name is mentioned (Adam, Noah, Abraham, David, Jonah, John the Baptist, Isa, or Muhammad), it is necessary that "peace be upon him" be added after mentioning his name.

Ramadan. An Islamic month of fasting from sunup to sundown. It is the ninth month of their lunar calendar, chosen by the first revelation of Muhammad given to Muhammad.

Ruah Allah. Arabic for *the Spirit* or *life-giving breath of God*.

salaat. *Prayers*, one of the five pillars of Islam.

Shokran lek. Arabic for *Thank you very much*.

surah. A chapter in the Qur'an.

thobe. *White robe* worn by Muslims that is usually tailored to fit as a dress shirt and goes all the way to the ankles.

Torat. The name given in the Qur'an for the Torah (Genesis through Deuteronomy).

Qur'an. The holy book of Islam that tradition says was given to the prophet Muhammad (PBUH). It contains roughly 65 percent biblical literature with more than fifty names, places, and events that are also in the Bible.

qurban. Arabic word for *sacrifice*; used to explain what God did for Adam, the ram provided for Abraham in place of his son, and what God performed with the person of Jesus.

Yehovah. The Hebrew word for the Creator. In other languages, the Creator is known as Allaha, Allah, Mungu, etc.

Zabur. The name given in the Qur'an for the writings of David (Psalms and Proverbs).

zakat. Obligatory giving, which is second in importance to prayer among the five pillars.

Talking about ISA

Appendix B

Paul's Message to the Athenians on Mars's Hill

Acts 17:16–32

(emphasis added)

[16] While Paul was waiting for them in Athens, his spirit was greatly upset because he saw he city was full of idols. [17] So he was addressing the Jews and the God-fearing Gentiles in the synagogue, and in the marketplace every day those who happened to be there. [18] Also some of the Epicurean and Stoic philosophers were conversing with him, and some were asking, "What does this foolish babbler want to say?" Others said, "He seems to be a proclaimer of foreign gods." (They said this because he was proclaiming the good news about Jesus and the resurrection.) [19] So they took Paul and brought him to the Areopagus, saying, "May we know what this new teaching is that you are proclaiming? [20] For you are bringing some surprising things to our ears, so we want to know what they mean." [21] (All the Athenians and the foreigners who lived there used to spend their time in nothing else than telling or listening to something new.)

[22] So Paul stood before the Areopagus and said, **"Men of Athens, I see that you are very religious in all respects.** [23] For as I went around and observed closely your objects of worship, **I even found an altar with this inscription: 'To an unknown god.' Therefore what you worship without knowing it,** this I proclaim to you. [24] The God who made the world and everything in it, who is Lord of heaven and earth, does not live in temples made by human hands, [25] nor is he served by human hands, as if he needed anything, because he himself gives life and breath

and everything to everyone. ²⁶ From one man he made every nation of the human race to inhabit the entire earth, determining their set times and the fixed limits of the places where they would live, ²⁷ so that they would search for God and perhaps grope around for him and find him, though he is not far from each one of us. ²⁸ **For in him we live and move about and exist, as even some of your own poets have said, 'For we too are his offspring.'** ²⁹ So since we are God's offspring, we should not think the deity is like gold or silver or stone, an image made by human skill and imagination. ³⁰ Therefore, although God has overlooked such times of ignorance, he now commands all people everywhere to repent, ³¹ because he has set a day on which he is going to judge the world in righteousness, by a man whom he designated, having provided proof to everyone by raising him from the dead."

³² Now when they heard about the resurrection from the dead, **some began to scoff,** but others said, **"We will hear you again** about this." ³³ So Paul left the Areopagus. ³⁴ **But some people joined him and believed.** Among them were Dionysius, who was a member of the Areopagus, a woman named Damaris, and others with them.

—NET Bible®

Notably missing in Paul's message to the Athenians, from an evangelical standpoint, is any quotation from his Bible. Paul had an equivalent to a PhD in the Old Testament, but never referenced it before a Gentile audience that did not recognize it as truth.

Appendix C
The *Adhan*, or Islamic Call to Prayer

God is the greatest (*Allahu akbar*); (four times)

I testify that there is no deity but God (*Ashhadu anna la ila ill Allah*); (twice)

I testify that Muhammad is God's Prophet (*Ashhadu anna Muhammadan rasul Allah*); (twice)

Come to prayer (*Hayya alas salah*); (twice)

Come to security / salvation (*Hayya alal falah);* (twice)

God is the greatest (*Allahu akbar);* (twice)

There is no god but God (*La ilah ill Allah);* (once)

optional line added for early morning salaat:

Prayer is better than sleep (*Assalatu khayrum minan naum*); (twice)

Talking about ISA

Appendix D
Opening Prayer
Surah 1 from Holy Qur'an

In the name of GOD,
    Most Gracious,
    Most Merciful,
    Praise be to GOD.
Lord of the universe,
    Most Gracious,
    Most Merciful,
    Master of the Day of Judgment.
You alone we worship,
    You alone we ask for help,
    Guide us in the right path.
The path of those whom You blessed,
    Not of those who have deserved wrath,
    Nor of those who have gone astray.

Talking about ISA

Talking about ISA

Appendix E
Qurban Poster

Talking about ISA

Appendix F
Qur'an Surah 37:100
Abraham and His Test of Faith

(emphasis mine)

"Oh Lord, grant me a righteous (son)!" So We gave him the **good news of a boy ready to suffer and forbear**. Then, when (the son) reached (the age of serious) work with him, he said, "Oh my son! I see in vision that I offer thee in sacrifice. Now see what is thy view!" (The son) said, "Oh my father! Do as thou art commanded: Thou will find me. If Allah so wills one practicing patience and constancy!" When they had both submitted their wills (to Allah) and he had laid him prostate on his forehead (for sacrifice), We called out to him, "O Abraham! Thou hast already fulfilled the vision!" Thus indeed do We reward those who do right. **For this was obviously a trial and We ransomed him with a momentous sacrifice.**

Talking about ISA

Appreciation

The fact that I'm writing these words on this page shows that many people have impacted my life, including a typing teacher and English language teachers (who wish I'd paid better attention). To list all those who compiled everything it took to arrive at these concepts would take most of the pages of this book. There are a several whom I must credit for helping me arrive at this place because the interactions you read would have never happened without them. The list is varied, and when you read them, you may find it hard to understand how their influence played a part. Rather than try to explain, I will merely say thank you…

Dr. Mark Young

Dr. Basil Younis

Jeff Hayes

Kevin Greeson

The Honorable, Mark Siljander

Nik Ripkin

Joseph Cumming

Safi Kaskas

Eli Stanley Jones

Some of them don't even know how they influenced me. Nearly all of them are listed because of what they *did* and less about what they said. Their actions allowed them to be powerful role models in my life. It is with sincere thanks that God brought each of them into my life when he did, and I'm grateful that they modeled boldness as well as lives worthy of being emulated in their service to the King of Kings.

Special thanks are due for Dr. Barry Leslie, Bill Phillips, and Craig Bess for suffering through very rough drafts to create a better product. And to Kelli Sallman for polishing the manuscript. I'm impressed by your ability to edit while maintaining my voice.

And last, but far from least—actually foremost—is my appreciation for my special Tamar. You take every part of me and make it better. Your tireless work made this what it is.